Techniques of Photography by AVAILABLE LIGHT

Colin Glanfield

Designed by
PHILIP CLUCAS MSIAD

Produced by
TED SMART and DAVID GIBBON

CHARTWELL
BOOKS. INC.

CONTENTS

INTRODUCTION

Photography has been the love of my life since my first VPK – acquired via a dubious trade while still at school during the war. With an f11 lens and the slow films then and when available, available light photography techniques became necessary even on the first roll. Coming from a family of keen amateur photographers, there was no shortage of the 'Taking better pictures' genre of books. Even though many dated from pre-World War One, the techniques remained the same. My father, having lost interest in still photography had nevertheless retained a cable release, a somewhat wobbly tripod and an Autoknips delayed action device. These became my first (and treasured) accessories. Grandfather refused to part with any of his gear, but did come up with a new exposure calculator. This device, made by the now defunct Johnsons of Hendon, required something like twenty factors to be dialled in and then by mathematically miraculous means, up came the exposure. Surprisingly, this tended to be near enough correct even for low light subjects on a dull winter's day indoors, though much credit must be given to the latitude of Kodak Verichrome and Ilford Selochrome of the period, together with the vigorous 'jungle juice' developer – probably a print developer – used by the local chemist for processing customers' films. Looking at some of these old D & P negs, with their high contrast and fog levels, I would reckon that all clients' films were given a three stop push as standard! This may have had something to do with the low contrast chlorobromide – or gaslight – printing paper used commercially at the time. Certainly when reprinting these old negatives some thirty years later, grade one paper is necessary.

My interest in available light pictures stemmed not only from necessity, but also from historical precedent. Grandfather, who by profession was a milling engineer, took photographs of his installations mainly for publicity use by his employers, but also for the joy of having his hobby subsidised by the firm. In the industrial premises of those days, just after the turn of the century, lighting levels were somewhat low. The usual technique was to set up the camera, open the shutter and go to lunch, returning from the meat pie and beer an hour later to terminate the exposure, hoping that the half plate had had enough. Development was by inspection under a red safe light in a staining pyrogallic developer. A kettle of hot water was used to give the emulsion suitable encouragement. Later exposure methods encompassed the use of magnesium ribbon as a light source, the exposure then being calculated in terms of inches at whatever aperture. The technique of lighting a factory interior from behind machinery (or pillars) out of direct line of camera sight is still used by industrial photographers today. Grandfather always felt that this method was somewhat dishonest, but then in those days employers were not as generous with time, and by using artificial light, several pictures could be taken in a single lunch break. Like all keen amateur photographers, my family did not cease to attempt pictures after the sun had gone down behind the left shoulder. Our family albums show sunsets, church interiors, seaside illuminations, winter storms, lightning over the hills, Christmas decorated front rooms, snow scenes at night, the cat asleep in Grandfather's favourite chair, Father as an angelic chorister in a local church, a paddle steamer engine room, and many other mementoes of long ago events and places.

As a professional photographer today owning the finest equipment money can buy, I wonder if something has not been lost along the way. Nearly sixty years' worth of difficult family subjects were to pass before the first 35mm camera with an f2 lens was taken into the family fold, and though there are still in existence some Autochrome, Finlay and Dufaycolor transparencies, it was the popularity of Kodachrome which finally brought this about. Grandfather continued to use his quarter plate Ensign with rollfilm adaptor, and invariably a tripod, until he died aged 89 years. He did not even approve of my Rolleiflex, as this made photography too easy. Perhaps he had a point, for a lack of equipment can be overcome by enthusiasm and technique, even in a subject as apparently difficult as photography by available light.

*Thanks largely to the introduction of a number of creative filter systems, soft focus and various other special effects have undergone a process of re-discovery amongst amateur photographers. The photographic image can be softened at both taking and printing stage, although the former practice is the more common. The degree of softness and overall effect depends on the system used, either purpose-made or improvised. **Right:** Backlighting is commonly used in conjunction with soft-focus effects, to further enhance the femininity of the subject. It is of course important to adjust exposure in such circumstances, or to ensure that adequate fill-in lighting is provided by using carefully positioned reflectors. **Facing page top:** The setting sun and a Winter mist created the atmosphere in this river scene. **Bottom:** Mirrors add to the feeling of space in interior shots.*

HISTORICAL DEVELOPMENT

HISTORICAL DEVELOPMENT: THE QUEST FOR SPEED

As long as there have been photographers, they have always asked for more, though unlike Oliver Twist, it has been for faster lenses and greater emulsion speed. In the early days this was not without good reason. We have all heard the stories of how daguerreotype photographers propped or clamped their sitters into rigid positions, so that a long exposure could be given. Assuming that bright daylight has not changed much since the 1840's, that the lens used was probably of f11 aperture, and that the exposure time was 8 seconds, then it is possible by extrapolating modern exposure data to arrive at an ASA rating for a daguerreotype! How does the thought of a sensitive material about 1/1000th the speed of Kodachrome 64 grab you? This is the sort of deal our photographic ancestors had!

As early as 1840, not long after the birth of a practical photographic process, a Viennese mathematician called Petzval became interested in the photographic exposure problems of daguerreotypists, and in consequence designed the first high speed photographic lens with an aperture of f3.4. In spite of the Petzval's limited coverage, the central definition was high, making it eminently suitable for portraiture, where a longer than normal focal length is preferred.

For the first forty-five years of its life, the camera went everywhere on three legs. It was only the advent of the fast gelatin emulsions of the 1880's, which, appearing on glass plates as well as in rollfilm form for Kodak's new $25 box camera, allowed hand-held instantaneous photography – under good lighting conditions – for the first time.

George Eastman's first rollfilm is stated in a contemporary book to have a speed of 75 H & D, which roughly translates as ASA 2.5. Theoretically, his film should have been around ASA 10 to have produced a snapshot image in bright sunlight, but then developers were somewhat fiercer in those days and a two stop 'push' not out of court.

The year 1890 produced the famous Goerz Dagor, a six element symmetrical lens of superb correction and covering power. The maximum aperture was f6.8, at which it was fully usable. 1895 saw the introduction of H. D. Taylor's Cooke Triplet, a lens which, perhaps more than any other design, paved the way to future exotica. Further improved emulsions in the 1890's allowed mass produced cameras, such as the $5 Pocket Kodak in 1895, the $10 FPK in 1897 and $1 Brownie Box in 1900. The age of the snapshot had begun.

For the more sophisticated, and the bicycle enthusiasts of the period, the hand and stand camera appeared, often with the new Bausch and Lomb pneumatic shutter, giving speeds of between 1 sec and 1/100 sec.

By 1900, dry plate speeds had reached new heights. One called the "Rocket" was of 250 H & D – or about ASA 8. Furthermore, it was orthochromatic, which meant it could cope with all colours apart from darker oranges and red. "Medium" speed emulsions were about ASA 3 and "ordinary" ones half this figure.

The famous Zeiss Tessar, which first saw the light of day in 1905, was a variation of the Cooke triplet design and for the first time brought 'speed' lenses of f4.5 aperture to the masses. Further development took the Tessar to f3.5 in 1908. Single and twin lens reflex cameras, from a slow start in the 1880's, began to appear in larger numbers after the turn of the century. SLR's with instant return mirrors – all done with gravity – were the order of the day by 1910 for both professionals and wealthy amateurs alike.

Small folding "Vest Pocket" plate and rollfilm cameras could now be equipped with f4.5 or even f3.5 lenses, allowing photographs to be taken under dull light conditions. Shutter speeds of up to 1/250 sec or more were commonplace.

1914 was memorable, and not only for the first 24 x 36mm format camera – the American Simplex. Its 400 exposure capability could well have lasted its owner through to the end of hostilities in 1918. Technology in the Great War period was more concerned with blowing people up rather than negatives, so that by 1920 the fastest plates were still only ASA 17.

The cinema industry, now spending more time indoors, required faster lenses. In consequence, Englishman H. W. Lee

Pentax ME-F aperture-priority automatic 35mm
SLR camera with full manual override,
fitted with 50mm fl.4 standard lens.

produced for the TTH/Cooke Company a design for the first f2 lens. It was called the Speed Panchro. Stemming from the Cooke triplet, this design (in modified form) is still with us today.

In the Fatherland, the first true available light pictures of a reportage nature were being taken by Dr. Erich Salomon with the famous Ermanox camera. Finally, in 1925, Oscar Barnack's 1913 Leica idea went into production. Two years later, A. O. Roth in England equipped it with interchangeable lens facility, fitting first a Meyer fl.5 Plasmat, then a series of Meyer telephoto lenses. The next milestone in camera design was the introduction of the 1932 Leica II and Contax I, both fitted with a coupled rangefinder. This was rather necessary for the 5cm f2 lens option on both cameras.

Top: **Erich Salomon,** *probably the first, and certainly one of the best known available light reportage photographers, took this picture of a group of diplomats at a banquet in the 1920s using an Ernemann plate camera,* **above,** *equipped with the then supremely fast f2 Ernostar lens.* **Left and top left:** *Attractive detail and interesting characters are to be found in abundance in the old English pub.* **Facing page top:** *Candles provide a mood of quiet intimacy, and can be used in many romantic situations.* **Bottom:** *An old cottage retains its feeling of warmth and homeliness when photographed by natural light.*

Top left: Room interiors taken *with wide-angle lenses frequently suffer from converging verticals. A carefully chosen camera angle, that takes into account the furniture as well as walls, will help minimise the effect.* **Top right:** *With light levels high and sky detail still visible, dusk is frequently considered a good time for 'night' shots.* **Left:** *Putney bridge over the Avon at Bath.*

Miniature camera users needed their fast lenses, as film speeds ranged from 4 to 12 ASA in daylight. Artificial light ratings were about half this. Rollfilm users had a speed range of 32 to 64 ASA. Advertised in 1934, the robot camera with its 24 x 24mm format on 35mm film, spring-driven film advance and compact dimensions, was much praised. Yet in its way, the Ihagee VP Exakta (1934 model) rollfilm SLR heralded much more, with its lever film/shutter wind and built in flash synchronisation terminals.

At the end of the decade, Ilford and Kodak were producing 100 ASA HP3 and Super XX respectively, in 35mm and rollfilm form. The Contax III, with built-in coupled photo-electric exposure meter and the world's first 35mm SLR with interchangeable lenses, the Kine Exakta, were on the market, together with many 35mm folding rivals to the Retina. Leitz had produced the clip-on clockwork Leicamotor with 2 FPS facility and Kodak introduced the large Super 620 with fully automatic exposure.

Before dismissing the thirties, mention must be made of the magazines written specifically for 35mm users which appeared in America, Britain and Germany. Most weekly and monthly photographic magazines vaunted a 35mm columnist, who inspired his readers with tales of photographic derring do in dark places. 'Life' magazine, and others, had a lot to do with this new enthusiasm.

The Kodak Ektra of 1941-46 was America's first quality 35mm camera and had interchangeable lenses, viewfinders and backs: about 2,000 were produced. The first postwar camera of note was the Contax S, the first pentaprism SLR with a pre-set iris diaphragm. Produced in East Germany in 1948 from early 1940's Zeiss Ikon plans and parts, this brilliant concept suffered from ersatz materials and poor assembly. The same year saw the introduction of the new Hasselblad 1600F, from, of all places, Sweden!

By 1948 all lens manufacturers were coating their products. The 1950's saw the first 'rare earth' designs and Japanese lenses by Nikon, Canon and Pentax were beginning to establish a fine reputation, f1.1 exotics by Nikon and Zunow were highly prized. By 1955 the faster films such as Super XX had reached 160 ASA whilst sheet film had achieved 400 ASA and Kodak's P2000 plate

500 ASA. The 1950's saw a rash of Leica copies from America, Britain and Japan. Leitz, always one step ahead, introduced the Leica M3 in 1954. The Japanese produced Canon and Nikon rangefinder cameras, in many ways the equal of the German opposition. Nikon produced an add-on electric motor drive (1956); Canon, a built-in trigger film/shutter wind; Pentax, the first instant return mirror (1954), later adding a pentaprism and semi-automatic stop down iris diaphragm mechanism. The famous Nikon F appeared in 1959, closely followed by the Canonflex. The first automatic exposure 35mm cameras appeared in Germany and Japan simultaneously.

1960's film speeds progressed rapidly, with 35mm Tri X at 400 ASA, Ilford's HPS at 650 ASA, HP4 at 400 ASA and Plus X/FP4 at 125 ASA. The sixties saw Canon's f0.95 'Dream' lens (1961), with many other manufacturers now offering f1.2 lenses for the first time. It was Leitz, Canon and Nikon who brought aspherics to the market, all three making very expensive f1.2 lenses with compound curves to give a degree of edge correction hitherto unknown.

1976 saw the introduction of Leitz' f1 Noctilux, an entirely new concept in ultra fast lenses, where contrast takes precedence over very high resolution. The other optical breakthrough has been in the use of moving elements – learned from zoom technology – to gain corrections whilst using a smaller number of elements and thus reducing costs and weight.

The last twenty years have really been the time for expansion of the colour photography market. Black and white technology produced Agfapan 1000 as a rival to Kodak's 650 ASA Royal X pan rollfilm. Kodak 2475/2485 recording films and Ilford HP5, together with Chromogenic Agfa Vario XL and Ilford XP1, bring the story up to date.

Facing page bottom right: The Kodak Super Six-Twenty of 1939, the world's first automatic exposure camera. Below left: Trains at Chicago's Union Station create a futuristic, tunnel-like effect. Below: The compactness of many modern cameras means that they can literally be carried at all times. Everyday scenes such as this are frequently avoided as photographic subjects, and yet they can often result in surprisingly striking shots. Look around you and try to see the potential in the activities that one normally takes for granted.

COLOUR MATERIALS

COLOUR MATERIALS

It is tempting to start a short history of colour photography from 1936. This was the year that Kodachrome and Agfacolor Neue subtractive processes were introduced in 35mm format, the former leading on to Ektachrome (via Eastman Aero Color film) and the latter to Agfacolor negative/positive, both in 1940. Whilst one can say that all modern processes evolved from this point in time, some of the theory is even older than photography and should at least be mentioned.

Right from the daguerreotype, there has been a demand from public and photographer alike for a colour representation of a subject. After all, painters have been using colour for a very long time, and though photography was remarkable in its ability to produce an accurate likeness at a fraction of the cost of a painted portrait, there was still the unfortunate fact that the image was black and white. Hand colouring of daguerreotypes began almost as soon as the process became available. Some artists, believing the famous dictum "From today painting is dead," took to painting oils so heavily over a daguerreotype that the original image was virtually destroyed. Later use of transparent colouring produced a more acceptable effect. Fox Talbot's contemporary pos/neg process, having a paper print as the end result, was more amenable to subtle hand colouring with water colours. Dye tints were extensively used during the later lantern slide, stereo and postcard crazes, with execution ranging from the crude to the realistic. Hand colouring continued right through to the 1950's. Indeed, sets of dyes are still available today, though now used for colour retouching and sometimes audio visual slides.

The theory of separating white light into three primary colours predated photography by some thirty years. It was not until 1861 that a young Scots physicist, James Clerk Maxwell, put his earlier theories into photographic practice, and produced the first colour photograph. This was achieved by making three negatives of the subject through a violet, green and red filter. Positives were then made and projected through the same filters

Top: What at first appears to be a moonlit townscape, is in fact a shot taken in the full light of day. Shooting into a sun carefully positioned behind a street lamp, the photographer avoided exposure compensation, thus reducing all objects to simple, dark outlines. The pattern of the highlights in the lapping water is indicative of a fast shutter speed.

Pentax LX aperture-priority automatic 35mm SLR camera with full manual override, fitted with 28mm f2 wide-angle lens.

with three lantern slide projectors so aligned as to give a registered superimposed final image. Considering that neither orthochromatic nor panchromatic materials were available at the time, it is not surprising that the world's first colour photograph appears somewhat murky.

In 1862, Frenchman Louis Ducos du Hauron, applying Gallic logic, designed a beam splitting viewer for the same purpose. Unfortunately he decided to use red, yellow and blue primaries – this being the "in" Gallic theory at the time. It took him seven years to work it out. Apart from this nationalistic blunder, Ducos du Hauron continued to research colour photography to such an extent that most of his writings were used practically at later dates.

In the 1870's and 1880's colour sensitivity to green and orange was developed. This enabled the tricolour enthusiasts to produce rather better results as long as they avoided red in their subjects.

The American, Frederick Ives, in the 1890's produced the first 'one shot' colour camera. This enabled three separation negatives to be made at the same time. He called his system "The Kromskop." This was derived from, or at least bore a passing resemblance to, the Ducos du Hauron machine. Ives produced commercial versions of his many inventions, including the first stereo colour photographs. Ready-made colour transparency sets under the trade name "Kromogram" were popular through to the early 1900's. Before going on the next stage in colour photography, mention must be made that three colour projection

*Simplicity is often the key to a successful photograph. A profusion of detail can prove visually distracting, drawing attention in different directions, and not leading the eye to a point of focus. **Facing page bottom:** Windows and arches are strong components in any picture, and can be used to frame a subject. **Above:** Straight lines have the effect of 'pulling' the eye, as shown in this shot of a lifeboat station backlit by the winter sun. **Left:** A powerful image created by the use of highlight and shadow.*

processes continued until as late as the 1936 Mikut camera and projector – which needless to say was a failure – therefore rare and now collectable!

Ducos du Hauron, and others, had experimented in the 1890's with fine ruled tricolour screens. These were either placed in front of the emulsion in contact, or were coated on to the plate and an emulsion coated over this. Either way, the camera's focusing screen needed to be reversed to allow for the additional thickness of glass. This made switching from colour to black and white a screwdriver job! The advent of panchromatic emulsions in 1906 made screen plates a more commercial proposition.

COLOUR MATERIALS

Once more in France (in 1904), the Lumière brothers – of ciné fame, came up with an idea for producing a screen plate. Instead of using ruled tricolour lines they experimented with very fine grains of potato starch, dyed red-orange, green and blue. Mixed together and randomly distributed over the plate, any 'white' spaces were filled with fine black powder. A panchromatic emulsion was then coated over this 'screen'. This unlikely sounding method worked. Launched in 1907 it became the first really practical system of colour photography.

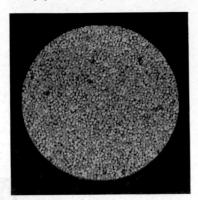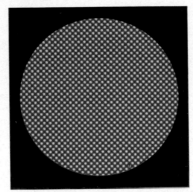

Above: Photomicrograph of the Lumière screen, composed of dyed starch particles, over which was coated a pan-chromatic emulsion. Launched in 1907, the system was the first *practical method of colour photography. Above right: Separate screens, used in contact with the film for both exposure and viewing, were the basis for several colour systems.*

Autochrome, as the process was named, needed a very light yellow filter over the lens to cut out excessive blue sensitivity. As mentioned, the camera's focusing screen needed to be reversed, though not long after introduction, a combined filter and correction lens was produced to obviate this. In spite of all the gold medals the Lumière brothers collected, their process had one snag – it was slow at about .25 ASA. Even photographers who were lucky enough to own an f4.5 'speed' lens, still needed a tripod for a ½ sec exposure, 'wide open', in sunlight. Needless to say, Authochromes were soon being taken of Paris at night, church interiors, winter scenes and so on. Autochrome survived in various faster forms such as Filmcolour (1931) and Lumicolor, until the late 1930's. Agfacolor plates of similar construction were made from 1916 to 1939. The later Agfacolor Ultra plate and rollfilm reached a speed of 2 ASA.

Ruled screen plates from many makers were marketed at the same time as Autochrome. Because a ruled screen stopped less light, they were anything up to eight times faster, thus enabling the first hand-held colour exposures to be made. Dufaycolor in 1934 was the first 35mm colour film. Though its ruled screen did not stand up well to projection, it was marketed until the 1950's. The Finlay (separate screen) process was even re-introduced in 1953 by Johnsons of Hendon in England. It lasted about a year and was used mostly by medical photographers.

Kodachrome and Agfacolor Neue are known as subtractive processes. For the sake of brevity, since both construction and processing are very complex, I will attempt a simple description. Imagine that an additive process is tiny red, blue and green filters, side by side, with a panchromatic emulsion underneath. It is termed additive because all three colours must be added together to make white. A subtractive process is best visualised as the same three filters, each with its own emulsion, and sandwiched together in a tripack. Processing involves bleaching out the primaries and the exposed silver, and replacing them by

Shown here is a magnification of the Finlay screen. Fast wide-angle lenses are ideal when photographing dimly lit interior scenes. Unfortunately, these are invariably expensive. As short exposures are often required, the only alternative is to use fast or uprated film.

COLOUR MATERIALS

complementary cyan, magenta and yellow dye images. The term subtractive comes about as any complementary colour must be subtracted from the white light falling on it. Another way of expressing this is that cyan is also known as minus red, magenta as minus green, and yellow as minus blue.

As stated, subtractive films have dye images when processed, thus, compared to the 'coloured' black and white images of an additive process, are much brighter when viewed. Due to the extremely thin tripack construction with three emulsions, they were four times faster (at ASA 8) than a screen plate, and sixteen times faster than the improved Autochrome and Agfacolor Ultra of 1936. It is perhaps worth noting that Kodachrome in 1936 was as fast as the contemporary Kodak medium speed 35mm emulsions – and with much finer grain. Kodachrome has improved in speed slowly over the years, through Kodachrome II of ASA 25 and Kodachrome X of ASA 64, to the current Kodachrome 25 and 64. Rumours of Kodachrome 200 persist.

Colour transparency technology progressed rapidly through World War II. Now that Agfa and Kodak had produced subtractive processes, their scientists were ordered and requested, respectively, to produce military versions. Agfa produced a negative/positive film and print process in 1942. Kodak, in the same year, produced Eastman Aero color – the forerunner of 1946 Ektachrome, Kodacolor and a domestic market system called Minicolor or Kotavachrome, for reversal colour prints from amateur or professional (sheet film) Kodachrome transparencies.

Japan's first subtractive reversal colour film was made by Sakura in 1940. Like the Kodak and Agfa product it was rated at 8 ASA. Postwar reparations meant that Agfa's technology was

available to all. Ansco, who already had a pre-war arrangement with Agfa, were the first to capitalise on this situation. Other manufacturers in the U.S.A., Britain, Germany, Italy, Belgium, Russia and Japan soon followed. In 1949, Agfa marketed their negative/positive process and Kodak introduced the orange masked Kodacolor. Film speed has risen from 8 ASA to the current 400 ASA stock. Aren't we lucky!

Colour printing processes merited learned tomes on the subject even as early as 1900. After all, colour separation negatives had been around a long time and so had a number of experimenters. Colour prints on paper were traditionally subtractive. From a set of tricolour separation negatives, a print was made of each (originally) upon semi-transparent (usually tissue) paper. This special bichromated paper was so treated as to eventually produce an image dyed in the colour complementary to the filter through which the original negative was exposed. The resulting cyan, magenta and yellow tissues (later 'gels') were then carefully superimposed upon a sheet of paper, and squeezed together. A domestic wringer was often used for this chore! Best known commercial versions of this carbro process were Sanger-Shepherd, Ives Hicro, Autotype Trichrome-Carbro, Jos-Pe and Eastman Wash-off Relief. The latter, replaced by Kodak's Dye Transfer process, is still in use today for special purpose prints and those intended for archival permanence. Needless to say, dye transfer print making is a highly specialised, labour intensive, and therefore expensive operation.

Production of separation negatives was originally done the hard way, with three separate exposures, three filters and three plate holders. It was not long before someone invented a sliding back with the filters over the plate. Even this was a bit slow for portraiture – remember each plate had to register exactly with the other two. Back to the drawing board, and once more Louis Ducos du Hauron (of tricolour fame), had worked it out first.

As previously mentioned, to American F. E. Ives must go the credit for producing the first beam splitter 'one-shot' camera. Tricolour cameras continued to be improved over the years. Probably the last to be made was the English Eves one-shot of 6 x 9cm or 5 x 4″ format, which was available until the late 1950's. Nowadays, separation negatives are made from transparencies by the original method, but using sheet film in special holders.

Additive techniques were tried for colour prints but without success. Both 'random' screens and ruled mosaics were too dense to give anything but a very dull print. Optimists even tried silver coated paper and translucent celluloid as a brighter base, but to no avail. Additive colour prints were not re-introduced after World War I.

Subtractive colour prints using a crude tripack appeared as early as 1916 (Ives) and reappeared in 1928 with Coloursnap (G.B.) and Ansco Coloral (U.S.A.). None of these processes lasted for longer than a year, so it was not until Kodachrome and Agfacolor Neue arrived, that the sophisticated colour print technology we have today became possible.

Spot meters measure the *intensity of light over a very restricted area. These are especially useful in situations of considerable lighting contrast, and whilst such expensive and sophisticated equipment cannot be justified for occasional use, the ardent theatre photographer may find the extra precision and control worthwhile.*

LENSES

EQUIPMENT LENSES

Nowadays there are very few really bad lenses. Compared with ten or twenty years ago, photographers have never had it so good. With the advent of the computer and high refractive index glass at reasonable cost, even a small maker can produce respectable lenses. Having said this, there can still be problems with poor lens element centering and mount quality, particularly when plastics are used. Even large manufacturers have been known to go through a period when production total has been given priority over quality control. Current high technology has produced simpler lens designs with fewer elements and no apparent loss of quality. Most standard focal length lenses of from fl.4 to f2 now only have six elements. This simplification of design stems from the researches of Leitz' Dr Mandler for two reasons. Leitz with the fl Noctilux took the route of higher contrast rather than definition, this giving apparently high resolution with colour materials. The second reason was in the design of a series of lenses using common elements. The calculations being comparatively simple by using a computer, the end result has been a reduction of production costs and, in turn, retail price. A third effect has been the ability to make wide

aperture lenses more compact because of a reduction in the number of elements. Ready availability of multicoating techniques has also helped.

One word about retail prices. The top manufacturers, such as Zeiss and Leitz, have a far higher rejection rate, which must be reflected in cost. This is not to say that other manufacturers produce an inferior product, but a high rejection rate can mean the difference between a very good lens and a brilliant one. The lucky photographers amongst us know a local dealer well and, in consequence, can try several lenses of the same type before selecting one as being the best of a batch. In truth, only those with a penchant for wall-sized blow-ups will notice the difference.

There are also those photographers who only seem to take photographs of test charts. Since you are, or are about to become, an available light photographer, which lenses should you choose? Assuming you can afford a 55mm fl.2 Aspheric, remember that such lenses, wide open, have so little depth of field as to be almost unusable at subject distances nearer than about 8 feet, unless, of course, ½" depth of field is all you want. For closer distances, my preference is to use a 35mm fl.4, even though most show a marked fall off in illumination towards the edges. This seldom matters when increased depth of field is more

important. The "framing" effect of uneven coverage can be used creatively to concentrate attention on the centre of interest – unless your subject happens to be a test chart!

In terms of construction, zoom and retrofocus (for SLR) wide angles have a lot in common, i.e. lots of elements, lower resolution unless stopped well down, low contrast, high distortion (barrel or pincushion) and flare, as well as a predilection for rendering a light source in shot as anything up to thirteen hexagonal images. Though I have been pretty damning about these lenses, particularly in relation to available light work, they still have their uses. For our purposes the modest maximum aperture of zoom lenses is somewhat limiting. Wide aperture retrofocus lenses from independent makers are usually awful, though Vivitar do produce some zoom and wide angle lenses which are better than many from famous camera manufacturers. The finest zoom lens I have ever used is the 35-70mm Zoom Nikkor, but in no way does it match a prime focal length lens from the same manufacturer. It is also – like all the others – a bit on the big and heavy side. My wife and son both own a 43-86mm Nikkor as their sole lens. Considering that this is one of the earliest zoom lens designs, and, as far as is known, has been little altered, its compact dimensions and adequate performance (for small colour prints) highly commend it. Unlike some modern 'independent' zooms of similar range, it does not suffer from bad distortion of straight lines of either the 'barrel' or 'pincushion' varieties. Many new zoom designs offer a macro facility, sometimes capable of producing adequate results, providing a small aperture is used. Likewise, the "matched multiplier" tele-converters offer a reasonable compromise. Full marks to the manufacturers for trying to achieve a multum in parvo lens, as obviously there is a demand for such an item. Maybe if we photographers were prepared to spend many times more on a universal lens, then we could get the performance the movie industry gets from its zoom lenses.

When it comes to telephoto and long focus lenses, there are fewer pitfalls, even when buying a "cheapie." Long focus lenses, as distinct from telephotos, use only a tiny portion of the potential coverage and therefore adequate results can be obtained. Using any long lens emphasises haze and flare, which can be misinterpreted as poor performance. A deep lens-hood plus a good multicoated Wratten IB type skylight filter can help a great deal. Camera shake can also be a problem with focal lengths of 300mm or more. Keep your shutter speed to 1/500 sec or less whenever possible. Use a heavy tripod for slower shutter speeds, or weigh down a lighter tripod with your camera bag or a string bag filled with rocks. When buying a long lens, make sure that it has a tripod bush somewhere near the centre of gravity when the camera body is attached and use this rather than the camera bush when fitting the outfit to a tripod. A cable or pneumatic shutter release is a must. A mirror lock-up facility on an SLR camera also helps.

New high refractive index glasses have brought forth a spate of wide aperture lenses, from 135mm f1.4 through 200mm f2, 300mm f2.8 and beyond. These beautiful, very expensive and heavy lenses are a must for the available light professional photographer, but out of reach for many others. If you are prepared to look around for a secondhand East German C.Z. Jena 180mm f2.8 or 300mm f4 "Sonnar" lens, these are good lenses at a budget price. They could be obtained with Pentacon Six, Pentax screw or Exakta bayonet mount. Any competent repair shop can adapt the latter two by using a standard "T" mount, though you will lose the automatic stop down mechanism if costs are to be kept at a reasonable level.

Macro lenses, though limited by modest maximum

Although colour temperature meters and correction filters can be used to adjust the response of film to most types of light, this is often undesired and impractical. The major problem with filters is that they reduce the effective film speed and hence necessitate greater exposure. Daylight films can be used under some forms of artificial light to give a pleasant warmth that we readily accept as natural. Whilst a blue filter could have been used to correct the 'cast' in these shots, such treatment would have destroyed the atmosphere.

apertures, do have the advantage of being computed for high corner resolution at maximum aperture. Though also designed primarily for close distances, in practice most show no sign of this, even used at infinity. Internal focusing of the elements in the latest 200mm macros allows reasonably short dimensions to be obtained. In spite of a higher cost than a comparable focal length lens, the macro design does save buying an extra lens for this purpose.

Catadioptric, or mirror lenses, now exist in 250mm and 300mm focal lengths with wider apertures than the traditional 500mm f8 and 1000mm f11 items. Outside of very special optics, the catadioptrics possess similar maximum apertures to long focus lenses. On the plus side, they are compact, but against this, the lack of an iris diaphragm means no control over depth of field. Whether you like an out of focus highlight being rendered as a "doughnut" is a matter of personal preference or expediency.

Teleconverters, like catadioptrics, also represent something of a compromise. Even the better six or seven element versions must lose 1½ to 2 stops of the prime lens' aperture; really need at least one to two stops shut down in order to pull in corner definition, and tend to lower contrast. Against these disadvantages, the compact dimensions of converters make them an ideal "get out of trouble" solution to some photographic situations. In black and white work it is better to enlarge a section of the negative.

One is frequently asked to compare camera makers' lenses with those from the 'independents'. As very few photographers, outside of those working for photography magazines, ever get to try most lenses from most manufacturers, one can only generalise. Usually, if both 'makers' and independent manufacturers' products are compared, the 'makers' lens will prove superior in two respects: wide open resolution and mount quality. Stopped down performance between the two is unlikely to show any great disparity unless the degree of enlargement is high. Mount quality is sometimes described as 'feel', though in practice only long and hard use is likely to show up differences. If initial cost is important, and the lens will not have an arduous life, then by all means buy an 'independent', but bear in mind that the ultimate re-sale value will be proportionately lower in percentage terms.

CAMERAS

Modern cameras I take to be anything up to twenty years old. Many of these like Canons, Leicas and Nikons can still use current lenses. Some, like the Mamiyaflex, Yashicamat, Hasselblad and others, have hardly changed over the years.

Many keen photographers have retained Rolleiflexes, Retinas, Pentax's, Minolta SLR's, Topcons, Alpas, Exaktas – you name it – as back-ups to the modern electronic wonder; simply because they cannot bear to part with them; as a second camera for colour negative or black and white; or because they slip in a pocket for travelling light. I know one professional photographer whose two new cameras jammed up on a long distance assignment. Whilst waiting for them to be sorted out he continued his work with a Rollei 35T. When the processed Kodachromes were returned, his editor could not tell which shots were taken on which camera. A high proportion of the Rollei shots were used in the book – some as double page spreads. This story has another aspect. The Rollei loaded with ASA 400 Ektachrome was also used for some available light shots. It had the advantage that subjects did not realise that the photographer was a "pro" and so took no notice of him, whereas if he had been loaded up with his usual outfit, reactions could well have been different.

Olympus OM 2n aperture-priority automatic 35mm SLR camera with full manual override, fitted with 24mm f2 wide-angle lens.

Facing page: The boiling waters of the Niagara Falls take on a vapour-like quality when photographed using a long exposure. These colourful, dramatically illuminated scenes were shot, without filtration, from the observation tower on the United States side of the Falls. *Left:* The round-the-clock operation of many heavy industrial plants means that dusk and night-time photography is possible. Dust particles in the air, lit from beneath by a setting sun, can create the most exciting and colourful sky scenes. Shown in this picture is the apparently deserted shambles of a Cleveland steel mill. *Below left:* The forbidding interior of a steel strip mill. The dim illumination provided by the small overhead lamps, is boosted by the rich glow of the white-hot steel disappearing into the shape-forming grip of the press. A rough knowledge of the various processes, or the assistance of a helpful guide, can prove invaluable in such industrial-type photography.

It has often been said that amateur photographers love gadgets. It has also been said that professional photographers are conservative. It may be that cameras are designed by engineers, not photographers. It is true that expensive cameras, made as a result of market research, do not sell, whereas a cheaper camera produced from the same background will. This year's wonder model will cause a slump in secondhand sales of the last wonder model. Then perhaps a year later the "oldie" will be fetching more money than the secondhand "newie." This has happened in recent years with the Pentax Spotmatic, various Nikkormats, Nikon F and F2, Leica M4 and M5, etc. I am surprised at the number of

photographers who have bought compact SLR's and later moved on or back to a traditional "large" SLR. I must admit doing the same, now owning Nikon F2, Canon F1 and Leicaflex R3 in the "large" category, as well as two Nikon FE compacts. I would also hate to be without my two elderly M2 Leicas.

Having said this, the bane of a professional's life is the question "What camera should I buy?" In return, I have to ask "What sort of pictures do you want to take?" and then attempt to find the extent of the questioner's photographic knowledge. Often, he or she will volunteer, "I was thinking of the new Super Junkflex. It only costs $200 in New York, complete with a super macro zoom and flash unit." My usual answer is "Don't." However tempting the Junkflex's specification and price, the chances are it will turn out to be a dog. When it goes wrong, there are no servicing or spare parts facilities: "Sorry, they stopped making this model." The trade-in value, even if it is still working, is nominal or nil. On the other hand, I know a lady who has owned a cheap Russian SLR for ten years, but she is gentle with mechanical things, only wants postcard sized prints and doesn't use the camera for more than a few films a year – rather like the proverbial school teachers who had twenty years use out of their Bolsey or Argus before falling for the blandishments of 126 Instamatics or 110 Ektras.

In the days of mechanical cameras one could advise a prospective camera owner to buy a Leica, Rolleiflex or Nikon and it would last him or her anything from twenty years to a lifetime. I recently met an elderly man who had just given up using his Leica after forty-five years – unfortunately as a result of failing eyesight. The camera had been serviced by Leitz every ten years at minimal cost since new. This camera had even been used professionally for ten years.

The biggest trouble with modern electronic cameras is batteries. According to a local repairman, more cameras are

Contax 137 aperture-priority automatic 35mm SLR camera with built-in motor drive, fitted with 135mm f2 Planar telephoto lens

wrecked by leaking batteries than by electronic or mechanical failure. Though the better makes of camera are modular, the cost involved with a cheaper model makes a repair uneconomical. Do take batteries out of cameras, motors and electronic flash units, even if it could only be a matter of weeks before you intend to use them again. Store batteries in a plastic bag, so that should they expire, you will contain their nasty effluents.

The other snag with electronic cameras is what happens when the battery goes flat. Yes, I know the pundits say "always carry a spare battery." I always do and I have had new spare batteries which were also dead, as well as a camera with a dead short in its circuitry, which leaves us with a useless single mechanical shutter speed of 1/90, or even worse 1/60 or 1/30 sec. I am glad that Pentax with their new LX recognise this problem and provide mechanical shutter speeds of B and 1/75 to 1/2000 sec. The Canon F1 replacement does likewise. In the meantime, there are still the Pentax K1000, Yashica FX3, Olympus OMI, Minolta SRT 101 and lots of "golden oldies" in good condition. The 2¼ square cameras present no problem in this respect, apart from the Hasselblad 2000 FC and the Bronica SQ, which might be termed "expensive paperweights" should the batteries fail.

Sadly, there is no such thing as a fully automatic camera. At some time or another the photographer is going to have to exercise judgement or be somewhat disappointed with his results. Perhaps this is best illustrated by the story of an Irish executive of a sister organisation – yes, he could have been Polish, Swedish or the subject of any ethnic story – but just happens to be Irish. However, he wished to purchase an automatic SLR for a trip of a lifetime to Hong Kong with his fiancée. Could I get him a suitable camera? Not knowing much about the automatic cameras available at the time, I phoned around and finally settled on the Pentax ME. He was delighted with the feel of the camera. I gave him a roll of Ektachrome to "waste" trying the Pentax out. He was very happy with the results and even I was impressed. After his trip he came to see me with the results – to complain! The camera was no good – "Look at these." Most of his street shots were under-exposed. I tried to explain that, since two-thirds of the subject was sky area, the camera would expose for sky and not skyscrapers. Then came the pictures of his fiancée silhouetted against a spectacular sunset. "I can't see her face," he complained and to prove his point he showed me a similar shot in a fashion magazine, where the "pro" had used fill-in flash. The next transparencies were of white painted buildings, except that they

Facing page: Two views of the San Diego skyline at night. Both shots were taken from the same view-point, using telephoto and wide-angle lenses. This page: *Moody London scenes. The misty atmosphere flattened the colours and gave the pictures a soft quality.*

were rendered as grey buildings against a very deep blue sky. Again, I tried to explain why this had happened. He was not convinced. "Have you read the instructions?" I asked. "Oh yes," he said, "it implicitly states that the camera gives fully automatic exposure under all lighting conditions, to give a perfect picture every time." I gave up at this point.

The sequel to this story is that he later traded the ME for an ME Super, which has both exposure compensation and manual override facility – I learned about this change of heart by accident.

Automatic focusing cameras can also have pitfalls. Photograph a single figure or a group of three people – no problem. Photograph two people standing apart and the sensor mechanism focuses through them on to the landscape or building behind, although all of these cameras have short focus lenses with sufficient depth of field (under good lighting conditions) to compensate. But what happens at f2.8 when the weather is dull? Hopefully the weather will turn a half stop duller still and up will pop the automatic flash. Yet automatic focusing cameras can be a boon, for taking grab shots of the kids playing, or at a party when focusing time can easily lose the shot. It's all a matter of "horses for courses."

Motordrives or winders operate at a speed of between one frame per second (cheap-o's) and eight frames per second (very expensive-o's). The human brain can stop movement in the order of 1/25 sec (or 16 frames per second in ciné terms). A ciné camera operates at 24/25 F.P.S. (1/60 sec) sound speed. Super 8 (sound) is 18 F.P.S. (1/30 sec). When taking portraits a motor drive (or winder) is useful, since you do not have to take the camera away from your eye to wind on. For sports or action work you are quicker than the quickest motor (unless you can afford a Hulcher. N.B. It also uses film at high speed and presumes its owner does not have a budget, overdraft or family to support.) and quieter. The slowest 35mm SLR's still operates at around 1/25 sec delay between mirror-up and shutter going across. Henri Cartier Bresson manages to produce "the decisive moment" without a motor drive. Do you really need one? Be honest with yourself about this matter.

CAMERAS

SMALL, MEDIUM AND LARGE FORMATS

There used to be a Royal Photographic Society definition as to what constituted a miniature negative size. This started from 2¼″ square downwards and was rigidly enforced by the British Customs and Excise for taxation purposes. Nowadays, most of us think in terms of 35mm and smaller as miniature; 6 x 4½, 6 x 6, 6 x 7, 6 x 9cm as medium; and 5 x 4 inches and up as large format.

The 6 x 4½cm format, which used to be known as 16 on 120 in the days when we counted numbers in little red windows, is a resurrected size becoming increasingly popular with amateurs, semi-pros and pros alike. It has the advantages over 35mm of better quality results, particularly with colour negative stock, and big enlargement capability in black and white. Larger than 35mm transparencies can be seen without a magnifier and are more saleable, they can be trimmed to super slide (1⅝″ square), and fit 10″ x 8″ proportions. Some 6 x 4½cm cameras have interchangeable backs and Polaroid facility.

Compared to 6 x 6cm cameras, these smaller format cameras are cheaper to buy and more economical of 120 (sometimes 220) film. According to one professional, the best shot always occurs on "frame 13" in his Hasselblad. Soon, no doubt, the same will be happening on "frame 16 or 17." In terms of size, the 6 x 4½cm cameras can be bigger than their 6 x 6cm rivals, when the optional anatomical grips and/or motor drives are added. As these cameras take both horizontal and vertical pictures, the grip sometimes is necessary for ergonomic reasons.

Just as with other formats, many professionals would like a camera which took upright pictures when gripped in the most comfy way, and as long as people, most books and all magazines are the same way up, this need will continue. After all, it used to be done with the 6 x 4½cm Super Ikonta and others. Any of you who have handled a Pentacon Six will know what I mean. How about it, Pentax?

6 x 6cm has been with us since the 1901 $1 Brownie Box camera and will no doubt continue to remain so. The camera is always held the same way up, albeit with a degree of film wastage, since very few people print pictures square any more, whereas in the early days of Rolleiflex popularity this frequently happened. Art directors and editors still like 6 x 6cm pictures, since they can be trimmed in different ways to suit various layouts. With some of the modern reprographic techniques using electronic scanning, transparencies are sprayed with a dulling medium. A 2¼″ square or larger transparency does stand some chance of being cleaned and re-used. A 35mm tranny has little or no chance.

The Hasselblad and some older Rolleiflexes give a choice of format, namely 6 x 6, 6 x 4.5cm and 4 x 4cm (or super slide). The latter has the advantage that it can be used in most good 35mm slide projectors where it utilises the entire screen area. This has particular application in Audio-Visual work, where a large amount of typographical information on a slide is more readable when projected. Rolleiflex, at one time, made a 35mm back. This was useful for portrait work, since the format was upright and the effective focal length a handy 75 or 80mm. Using only the central

Left: A cross-screen or star filter was used for this shot of the cabaret performer. These attachments consist of a clear, optically flat glass or resin sheet with lines etched on the surface to produce patterned flare from reflections and point-sources of light. Four, six and eight point *star effects are the most common. Because of their tendency to soften the image, these filters are sometimes useful for portraiture, adding sparkle to any jewellery worn by the sitter. Above: A hand-held, wide-angle shot of the stage at the Everyman Theatre, Liverpool.*

resolution of the lens, print quality was as high or higher than an equivalent lens made specifically for a '35' of the period.

A 6 x 6 / 6 x 4.5 / 4 x 4cm format with 220 film gives a shooting capacity of 24, 30 or 32 exposures – approaching 35mm loading capacity.

Fujica AX-1 aperture-priority automatic 35mm SLR
camera, fitted with 28mm f1.9 wide-angle lens.

Medium format cameras do suffer from comparatively slow lenses, though maximum apertures have crept up, from f2.8 to f2.4, f2 and even in one case to f1.9. 6 x 7cm format cameras have lenses of from f3.8 to f2.4 maximum aperture. Only the delightful Plaubel 67 has a wide angle f2.8 lens as standard equipment. Whilst these maximum apertures may seem a disadvantage, a modest one stop push effectively doubles the lens speed. The resulting tranny or neg is still about 4x (6 x 6cm) or 5x (6 x 7cm) larger than 35mm, with a consequent reduction in granularity pro rata.

The in-between format of 6 x 9cm (or 8 on 120) should be more popular than it is since it aesthetically matches our beloved 24 x 36mm. The range of cameras available is still reasonably large, whether one is thinking of venerable Super Ikontas, "Baby Graphics" or Mamiya 23's, new monorails and hand/stand cameras. Here you have a choice from the functional, budget priced Galvin to the superlative Linhof. Few of these cameras are suited to available light work – at least, not off a tripod – though the large format f2.8 Zeiss Planar is available at a price. 6 x 9cm

seems to find favour particularly with Industrial photographers, as a convenience/quality compromise, where camera movements are necessary, roll film magazines/Polaroid facility is useful, and there is an easy transition from 6 x 9cm to AV work – or a poster sized blow-up.

5 x 4 and 5 x 7 inch cameras have found favour with the backpack fraternity, now that the traditional folding plate camera of yore has appeared in new guise. Available light work in large format is mostly restricted to landscapes, both urban and rural, and to some very impressive portraits and nudes, often taken under light conditions which only those with a sixty-year memory could remember. A few enthusiasts do the same thing with 10 x 8" format cameras, when an assistant or a class of students comes in useful but is not obligatory. A tripod is.

If you want to be sure of getting some well-exposed shots of a stage-show but, because of contrasty lighting, are unable to trust your meter readings; *bracket each exposure and if possible note the details, as this will help you build-up experience for the next time.*

FILM

FILM

A large number of available light subjects are of high contrast, so it is therefore to our advantage that high speed colour and black and white emulsions are of a lower contrast than their slower stablemates. Against this, the high speed emulsions are grainier. Pushing development increases both granularity and contrast. So with these Murphy-like parameters, which film should one choose?

For physical reasons, granularity is lower with black and white film than with either colour negative or transparency films of the same ASA rating. A 10 x 8″ print from a 35mm black and white 400 ASA negative will be perfectly acceptable, but one from a 400 ASA colour negative film will not be, particularly if the subject contains large areas of even tone. Projected 35mm transparencies from 400 ASA films may be acceptable providing they are not mixed with, say, Kodachrome. The texture of a beaded screen and the nature of projection lenses will help disguise granularity – as may the subject matter! The screens used in reproduction processes tend to smooth out grain too, particularly the coarse screens used in the newspaper industry.

When making an exposure on any film of any type of any speed, there is one cardinal rule. If in doubt, over-expose on black and white and colour negative stock, and under-expose on colour transparencies. This way, you have a chance to save your shot. You can always print through a thick negative, or dupe a dense transparency for an acceptable result. The other way, you cannot put in what is not there.

BLACK AND WHITE

35mm black and white materials are available in a selection which ranges from the virtually grainless Adox KB14, of only 20 ASA, to the very grainy Kodak 2485 ASA 5000 – 8000 recording film.

At the lower end of the speed scale, films like Adox KB14 and 17, Agfapan 25, Ilford Pan F and Kodak Panatomic X – the fastest being only ASA 50 – are a must for resolution when this is of paramount importance. These slow emulsions are of higher contrast and, in consequence, need a softer working developer such as Kodak Microdol X if gradation is necessary. Unfortunately, this type of developer is not very "active," resulting in anything up to one whole stop loss in emulsion speed. However, for ultimate results in 35mm work, there is really no other choice.

Assuming that – like in life – one must compromise most of the time, the medium speed films like Agfapan 100, Adox KB 21 (100 ASA), Ilford FP4, Kodak Plus X and Verichrome Pan (all 125 ASA) are the best films for general use. It is hard not to get an acceptable result, no matter what developer is used. My own preference is for Ilford FP4, which I firmly believe to be the finest film in the world. It copes admirably with careful use or professional abuse. Agfapan, Adox KB 21 and Kodak Plus X are really extensions of the ultrafine grain group, and perhaps should be treated as such in processing. Gradation is not as good as with FP4, though granularity is probably finer. Verichrome Pan is the ideal snapshot film with a reputation for exposure latitude that extends over many many years. Granularity is higher than in other medium speed films, which perhaps explains the latitude aspect. Verichrome Pan will stand everything thrown at it and still produce very acceptable results, provided a high degree of enlargement is not envisaged.

High speed black and white emulsions have become even more popular with amateur and professional alike, since Kodak first broke the 400 ASA speed barrier with their Tri-X film some eighteen years ago. Even more years before this, Kodak set the

same precedent with the Super X and Super XX, though the granularity of these earlier films was only really acceptable to the gentlemen of the Press. The old Ilford HP4 and HPS were never in the same league as Tri-X, albeit good films in their own right. The comparatively recent HP5 is a different kettle of fish, being, in the opinion of many, superior to its Kodak rival, both in gradation and, in consequence, "pushability"! Outside of mainland Europe, Agfapan 400 has never gained the reputation (or market share) it deserves. I have never met a poor Agfa product – even Agfapan 1000 was right for its intended purpose. One can only assume this situation has something to do with the power of advertising or a strong home market. The wide acceptability of ASA 400 films for general use has brought about a situation whereby several camera makers now offer a top shutter speed of 1/2000 sec, and

Most photographers under-stand the term 'available light' to encompass only those situations where light levels are awkwardly low. The definition does, however, include daylight *and any light that the photographer uses as found, without adding to it. Available light photography is not restricted only to the night-owl.*

FILM

neutral density filters have become common items in the gadget bag. For some exposure situations, 400 ASA is just too much!

A newish technique used by amateurs and professionals alike is to rate a fast film at 200/250 ASA (a prime speed rating which does not exist in black and white film) and then either cut development time or use an ASA speed reducing ultra fine grain developer to compensate. The resulting negatives have excellent gradation and slightly reduced granularity. The similar proposition of using diluted developers will be covered in a later chapter.

This top end of the ASA scale now includes the new chromogenic Agfa Vario –XL and Ilford XP1, both with a top speed rating of up to ASA 1600. These remarkable new films owe more to colour negative technology than anything gone by. Indeed, the Agfa film is C41 compatible. The Ilford film is only unofficially so, better results being obtained by using its own special processing chemicals. The gradation and grain even at ASA 1600 are a near match to that of ASA 100-125 medium speed films. There are unfortunately the drawbacks of high chemical costs and processing temperatures, together with a negative which takes about twice as long to print, due to film base colouring. From an ecological or commercial point of view, the possibility of silver recovery is a plus factor and points the way to future trends. The probability of having both colour and black and white negative stock processed in the same chemicals at the same laboratory, even the technical feasibility of printing both black and white and colour images on the same high speed printer on the same resin coated colour stock, must be an attractive proposition to processing houses.

When it comes to 120 rollfilm or sheet film sizes, there is about the same range of emulsions available. The one exception is the lack of chromogenic Agfa or Ilford sheet film for the present! There are, however, 1250 ASA emulsions, like Kodak's Royal X Pan, which though grainy, become more usable as negative format increases.

Humble f3.5 and f2.8 lenses become in effect f2 and f1.7 respectively when a 1250 ASA rating is compared to that of 400 ASA. Even an f5.6 lens on a 5 x 4", 5 x 7", or 10 x 8" camera in turn becomes an effective f2.8 (Tri-X sheet film is rated at 320 ASA) and who cares about grain on a 10 x 8" negative!

Large format film can also be push processed with fewer side effects compared to smaller formats. Any resulting excess contrast can be compensated for by printing with the cold

cathode enlarger heads, normally fitted to large format black and white enlargers.

It is worth mentioning that fast orthochromatic sheet film is available for those subjects where red sensitivity is not important. Though becoming a lost art, the technique of development by inspection under a safelight – as distinct from time and temperature – has a lot to commend it, particularly for subjects like landscapes and interiors. The other bonus is the ability to process a series of shots negative by negative, without the inevitable "averaging" of rollfilm processing.

COLOUR

Colour transparency materials vary in speed from ASA 25 (Kodachrome) to ASA 400 (Agfa, Fuji, Kodak, Sakura and others). At the lower end of the speed table, Kodachrome 25 has many adherents. Professional photographers have used this ultra fine grained film for shots intended for 48 sheet posters! It is still the sharpest transparency film ever produced and the standard

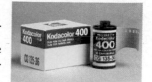

Kodacolor 400. 400 ASA daylight-balanced colour negative film. Available in 110, 35mm and 120 rolls.

by which other films are judged. Unfortunately, the capital cost of setting up a Kodachrome processing plant is extremely high and needs a very high throughput to justify its financial existence. Processing time is longer and "push" facility only available in the USA. Whilst Ektachrome and others are getting nearer to Kodachrome in quality, they still have a long way to go, particularly in archival terms. Let's enjoy it while we still have the chance.

Most colour transparencies taken by photographers are in the ASA 50-100 speed category. Ektachrome 64's are probably the most popular, with Agfachrome and Fujichrome having a strong home market. Any non-Kodak transparency film has a hard time establishing itself, simply because processing facilities cannot exist in the same numbers. Some manufacturers have gone the route of paying E6 royalties to Kodak to ensure comparable processing facilities for their product. In general, Kodak operate a virtual monopoly throughout the world, though many photographers are beginning to appreciate the virtues of the characteristics shown by other makers' products. In particular, the dull weather subject rendition of both Agfachrome and

The sky, whether clear, misty or laden with clouds, is a powerful creative force in outdoor photography. It can be used to transform the nondescript scene into a dramatic one. Exposure should be carefully considered when showing a large expanse of sky.

Fujichrome is becoming more accepted as an 'improvement' over Ektachrome. Landscape photographers especially find a non-Kodak rendering more pleasing. Kodachrome 64 of course fits into this ASA speed range. I have never been able to understand the strong feelings expressed over this film. For some inexplicable reason it falls into the "hate it or love it" category. My own view is that Kodachrome 64 sometimes has a tendency to render black as somewhat greenish, but in no way can this be considered unacceptable. The characteristic Kodachrome 'bite' is still apparent.

High speed colour films in the 160-400 ASA category tend again to be a Kodak province. The late lamented GAF 500 for

once took away the Kodak laurels. This film was grainy as hell but in the hands of some professional photographers produced incredibly beautiful Renoiresque effects. Had this pictorial use been better publicised and processing facilities more widely available, perhaps GAF 500 would still be with us. Kodak's other rival in the 400 ASA stakes is Fujichrome 400. Having used this film, I feel that it has much to offer. Assuming that one has the facility to carry an additional camera body, the contrast and colour differences between Fujichrome 400 and Kodak EL 400 can be used to advantage. Preference for colour rendering is of course a subjective matter, though this becomes less controversial as light levels become lower. Until recently, only

Fujichrome 400. 400 ASA daylight-balanced colour transparency film. Available in 35mm size only.

Agfa and Kodak produced reversal colour films specifically balanced for tungsten illumination. Both manufacturers' products, although technically balanced for a 3200° K light source, are in practice very forgiving to those who stray from the straight and narrow. As most photographers (and people) prefer a warmer subject rendition, even shots taken in domestic lighting with orange lampshades, will still bring forth ooh's and aah's from the family when projected. The newly announced 3M colour slide 640T film has an impressive 640 ASA rating for tungsten light. Though nominally balanced for 3200° K, the film is stated to give pleasing results with light sources from 2850° K (domestic lighting) to 3400° K (photofloods). 3M have stated that acceptable results can be obtained by pushing to ASA 1280. Standard Kodak E6 processing is used.

One cautionary word about transparency films. There is a tendency to use 'professional' rather than 'normal' Ektachrome film in the expectation of getting better results. If you shoot and process in the same day, then this is true, but 'professional' Ektachrome is not designed for snapshooting across a long period or for taking on holiday to somewhere hot. Kodak make 'amateur' Ektachromes specifically for these purposes, as well as Kodachrome. Agfachrome and Fujichrome as well as the 3M/Ferraniacolor films are also tolerant in this respect.

Rollfilm colour transparency material follows the same pattern as its smaller relatives. Unfortunately, Kodachrome is not available in 120 size, though many years ago it was made in sheet film sizes. Large format users have only a choice of Agfachrome or Ektachrome, balanced for daylight or tungsten lamps, and of ASA speeds between 32 and 64. At one time, we also had 160 ASA High Speed Ektachrome, which is rumoured to be returning in E6 guise. For those of us who undertake available light large format photography – like car photography at dawn – it cannot arrive too soon.

35mm format colour negative films are available from a far wider number of manufacturers, this being the growth market. They range in speed from Agfacolor at 80 ASA through the 100/125 ASA range to the 400 ASA films, the latter two categories being produced by the famous names as well as the myriad of 'own name' brands, many of which emanate from Japan, Italy, East and West Germany. Virtually all colour negative stock is now compatible with the Kodak C41 processing chemistry, so if your cassette of "Funnycolor" is not marked C41, then check with your local lab who should keep a list and will advise you accordingly. An acquaintance of mine processed a roll of Russian colour negative film in C41 chemicals (with no dire effects), after being turned down by several labs for chemical rather than political reasons. At the time of writing, Kodak's Vericolor II (ASA 125) is far and away the best colour negative film on the market – in terms of fine grain and gradation – though is more critical in exposure terms. Kodacolor II, essentially a snapshot film, has the greatest exposure latitude. Of the 400 ASA group, both Sakura and Fuji films have an increasing number of devotees, Kodacolor 400 is undoubtedly the market leader and Agfacolor CNS 400 probably has the finest grain and gradation – certainly, its rendition of skin tones is very good.

120 rollfilm users, once more, have a smaller choice. Fujicolor having joined Agfa and Kodak in this market, there is now a choice of ASA 80, 100, 125 and 400 films, with Kodak's Vericolor II available in 220 length as well as 120, balanced for artificial light or daylight.

Sheet film users are limited to Agfa and Kodak products of 80 and 100/125 ASA respectively. Both makers produce an emulsion balanced for either daylight or tungsten light. The rather grainy ASA 400 emulsions would be welcomed if produced in sheet film guise, for reasons already stated.

Before moving on to instant picture materials, perhaps a word about ISO speed ratings. These can best be described as yet another example of bureaucratic barminess. An ISO rating simply combines both ASA and DIN settings, which previously were printed on most manufacturers' products anyway. Instead of ASA 64/DIN 19/10°, we now have ISO 64/19°. Enough said?

*Facing page bottom: Two differently exposed shots taken in the same restaurant; one to capture the view from the window, the other showing the interior setting. The interior of Au Printemps, **above and facing page top,** the Parisian department store, is much photographed on account of its architectural splendour.*

INSTANT

Instant picture material, now generically known as "Polaroid" by the great general public, much to Kodak's annoyance, has been with us for over thirty years from Polaroid, and rather less from Kodak, who only produce a single 150 ASA colour material in direct rivalry to Polaroid's Time Zero SX 70 pack. How many photographers actually produce available light pictures on instant film, as distinct from using adaptor backs on medium or large format cameras for exposure checking, is a matter for conjecture.

Certainly some very good portrait work on colour 'instant' has appeared in the photographic press. One magazine devotes a regular column to instant pictures, so perhaps this is an expanding interest. Polaroid make black and white positive/negative materials of ASA 75 speed, black and white print only, from 400-3000 ASA, and various specialised high-contrast and transparency versions. Formats go from SX 70 via nominal ¼ plate and 5 x 4" sizes to 10 x 8" and beyond. In spite of the advantage of instant "enprint" sizes, the hardware is large and sometimes heavy. One suspects that the immediacy of instant pictures is a novelty that rapidly wears off. Professionals now find that Polaroid is habit-forming, both for themselves and their clients. There is even a growing number of 35mm photographers seeking the older Polaroid cameras with adjustable shutter speeds and apertures, which are used for checking lighting set-ups as well as exposure.

EXPOSURE & METERING

EXPOSURE AND METERING

What is correct exposure? Unless you photograph test charts, this is a subjective matter. Take half a dozen quality cameras and photograph the same subject under identical conditions with each. The chances are that perhaps two of the six will give matching results. This occurs for several reasons. The manufacturer may prefer a lighter or darker transparency. One maker's metering pattern may be more centre-weighted than another and his light sensitive cell may be more or less sensitive to some colours. In my experience, both the Leicaflex and Nikons which I own give transparencies that are consistently ⅓ stop dark, which is how most professionals and blockmakers like them. On the other hand, when using colour negative film, I prefer a slightly dense negative, which my old Pentax delivered every time. This, of necessity, means that the fussy will have to cheat their film settings to get what is needed. The other problem lies with Ektachrome (and other) processing labs. I once sent five identically exposed rolls of film to five labs, not for the sake of research but because we were looking for a new lab. The results were totally dissimilar, with about a stop in density variation and colour casts of all hues. In truth, none of the labs' work was unacceptable, providing that studio filtration and exposure was suited to the processing. With less knowledge, we could have blamed a camera. We finally chose the lab that matched nearest to the one we had used previously, just for consistency.

There is still a choice of "match needle," LED's in various forms, mechanical needles or liquid crystal readouts in view through the camera viewfinder eyepiece. Some of these apply also to medium format cameras. For the available light photographer, there is a lot to be said for an LED readout – it avoids using a torch or clip-on supplementary scale illuminator.

There is also a lot to be said for using a shutter preferred exposure system, whether your camera is automatic or not. Most of us know the lowest speed at which we can avoid camera shake. This is particularly important with match needle systems, as it is all too easy to produce a perfectly exposed blur. The Nikon EM automatic incorporates a bleeper to let you know when the shutter speed is getting too low for safety. At first I found the bleeper infuriating, but have now learned to live with it. When taking pictures under dark conditions and using a camera with needle read-out, it is possible to hold a piece of white paper, or your hand, just in shot when metering, in order to see what is happening.

Exposure compensation facility, for holding shadow detail in against the light pictures, is a feature which all cameras have had to some degree, whether it has been a separate indexed control ring or simply using the ASA speed settings. Several new cameras have reduced this function to a simple push button, giving an effective one stop or two stop exposure increase. The "one stop" system tends to be better for colour transparencies, the "two stop" being rather drastic, though fine for colour negative or black and white pictures.

Some mention should be made of the characteristics of the light sensitive elements in a meter/metering system likely to be encountered by photographers. The original selenium cells, developed in the late 1920's and early 1930's needed no batteries. The action of light upon the cell surface generated a tiny voltage which could be measured by a delicate microgalvanometer, in order to give a needle reading across a scale. The sensitivity of the meter could be increased by doubling the cell area with a clip-on "booster", which gave rise to house-brick sized movie meters in the early days. The selenium cell needed an acceptance angle of up to 180^0 with a glass or plastic light concentrating screen added. Colour sensitivity was rather better than current

Despite the fact that ballet, as an art form, appeals to a strictly limited audience, images of the ballet class are inexplicably popular. For some strange reason, photographers and *painters alike are inspired by such scenes, and sometimes achieve fame by portraying them. Whatever the reasons, pictures such as these are undeniably attractive.*

Weston Master V selenium cell exposure meter. Despite its limited sensitivity, this popular meter set the standard by which all others are judged.

Available light and ballet *form a particularly attractive visual partnership. Interpretation of the subject is of course individual, however, soft focus devices are commonly employed to enhance the delicate charm of such scenes. This, together with a slight degree of over-exposure creates an airy feel and helps diffuse the colour in an impressionist manner. Fast film, pushed a stop or two, will show an increase in grain that adds to the painterly quality.*

cells. Selenium cell meters in cameras were widely used until the introduction of Cadmium disulphide (Cds) cells in the early 960's. As far as I know, only the famous Olympus "Trip" still uses elenium in a current camera. I have a 1932 Metrawatt selenium) Leicameter which still works adequately enough for lack and white photos, as also does its 1935/6 Weston ounterpart.

The transistor revolution of the 1960's brought about the introduction of Cds light sensitive cells. By adding battery power, it was possible, through the use of transistors, to measure current variations between cell and battery, amplify the compact Cds cell's tiny output, couple this to a stronger/steadier micro-ammeter, and translate the whole into photographic terms, with greater light sensitivity, and vastly more compact dimensions

EXPOSURE & METERING

than the previous selenium systems. Once a lightly loaded battery was in the camera, its surplus capacity could be put to use to power LED's and electronically controlled shutter mechanisms. This trend has continued into the use of bigger batteries, which now may have to cope with built-in motor winders, electronic flash and autofocus mechanisms.

The disadvantage of Cds cells is their comparative lack of colour sensitivity, a situation which has been improved upon by the GASP cells of the late 1970's. Also known as Silicon Blue, these gallium arsenide/silicon phosphate cells were a product of the Silicon Valley revolution. Their reaction time to a light pulse is fast enough to allow in-camera metering of an electronic flash. They have a higher spectral sensitivity, though camera manuals should give warnings about the use of orange, red and (for a different reason) polarising filters with a TTL measuring system. This is usually in the order of increasing exposure by one stop for an orange, and two stops for a red filter, over indicated exposure. Cds cells have one large disadvantage known as "memory". If, for instance, a picture was taken in bright light, the camera then

taken indoors and another picture taken, the indoor picture would be under-exposed because a percentage of the outdoor reading would be retained by the cell. Within my experience, the Cds "memory" could be anything from a few minutes to half an hour, largely depending upon the quality of the circuitry involved.

Spot or average metering? With several more expensive cameras now offering this choice, which should one use for available light shots? The hand-held spot meter, measuring an area of anything from $\frac{1}{2}^0$ to 3^0 has been used by professional movie makers for many years and professional "still" photographers for not so many. The disadvantage of spot metering is that the photographer has to exercise considerable judgment in choosing exactly the right area to meter from, and with a $\frac{1}{2}^0$ or 1^0 meter it is all too easy to get it wrong. My Leicaflex has a simple switch from spot to average, which can be actuated without taking the camera away from the eye. If I have any doubt as to whether my spot reading is from the correct area, I can note the readout, switch to averaging mode, and bracket exposures

Facing page: Ektachrome 160 tungsten film was uprated by two stops and used together with a diffusion filter to produce these dream-like shots. Pushing the transparency film led to an increase in contrast and a consequent loss of shadow detail, further enhancing the ethereal quality. There is more to ballet than just the dancing, and it is valid to try to capture some of the peripheral activities: the backstage preparations and the scenes of physical and mental exhaustion of the highly dedicated artists, **left and top left.** *Spare the feelings of your subjects, however, and call the longer lens into use to get the meaningful shot.*

between the two readings if there is any great discrepancy. I seldom have to do this as the Leicaflex spot is of generous size – about 5% of screen area, regardless of the focal length of lens used. Most averaging meter systems are "centre weighted," albeit with varying measurement patterns and efficiency. In practice most work well, only being fooled by very bright or dark subject foreground area, or light sources "in shot."

EXPOSURE & METERING

It is somewhat unrealistic to expect the management of a major theatre to allow amateur photographers access to a performance, or even practice session, by a prestige ballet company, when passes for the professionals are often strictly limited. This should not, however, discourage would-be ballet photographers from pursuing their interests at amateur shows, where performers and management alike are usually amenable and invariably eager to obtain copies of publicity-type shots in exchange for photographic facilities. By carefully choosing your moment, and showing the more appealing and polished poses, results can often be as effective and 'professional' as those taken at a performance by a renowned company.

Programmed exposure measurement is now offered as an optional mode on some expensive SLR's. Previously the province of cheap cameras, it allows the user mindless freedom from worry about any exposure calculation. The range is in the order of from 1/30 sec at f1.4/f2.8 to 1/1000 sec at f16/f22, going from dull to very bright exposure conditions respectively. Rather as with automatic transmission in a car, I often wonder who is in charge!

The much loved Weston (selenium photo-sensitive cell with good colour sensitivity, and no need for batteries) will hopefully be with us for a long time yet. I know several cinematographers who will buy up Weston meters with alacrity, in order to ensure a supply of spares or spare meters for the future. They tend to be the guys who take rubber boats up the Amazon or climb mountains – situations where battery shops or Ni-Cad charging facilities are rather unusual. For the same reason they also tend to own numbers of clockwork Bolex 16mm movie cameras. But perhaps I labour the point!

The situation regarding hand-held spot meters is that they tend to be complicated and expensive! They are mostly produced by sophisticates already in the camera/lens field, such as Pentax, Minolta, Soligor, and Sekonic. It may seem like talking down, but they are best suited to photographic experts, preferably with a capital E. Otherwise it is a matter of application, wasting lots of film, oblique, copious notes, and a good memory, before you can learn to love them. They are also likely to be damn near as big as your favourite compact SLR.

Incident light measurement, or measurement of the light falling upon, as distinct from light reflected by the subject, was a theme developed by an English genius, P. C. Smethurst, in the middle 1930's, primarily for cinematographers and colour workers. His findings gave rise to the 1938 AVO-Smethurst High-Light exposure meter, a selenium instrument with a fixed translucent glass over the cell. A comprehensive booklet gave instructions in the use of this meter. Supplied, were gummed stickers stating "Please give uncompensated processing to this film." Nowadays, incident light measurement is the province of hand-held meters, though some old cameras like the Retina and M2/3 Leicas were supplied with a clip-on plastic attachment. Favourite incident meters are the Weston (with Invercone attachment), Lunasix/Lunapro and lately the Calculite, though the classic Norwood Director and its updated 'descendant' the Sekonic L418, have their devotees. The Lunasix/Lunapro and Calculite have a prodigious low light level measuring capacity, far-exceeding anything built into a camera, so for moonlight or night shots…

In rough and ready terms, an incident light meter gives a figure similar to a reflected reading from a 20% grey patch or skin tone, which is probably the best way to average out an exposure. Here, the colour of the subject is immaterial. On a Weston meter, the A-C and U-O markings give the theoretical maximum range of tones capable of being handled by colour and black and white films respectively. This gives the user the chance to take several readings from his subject and place the final exposure between settings, or at either end, dependent upon the range of subject brightness. This is the famous zone system of Ansel Adams, which has produced probably the finest black and white print quality ever seen.

In terms of subject range of luminosities, I would lift from the Classic L.P. Clerc some of the following:–

	Range
Landscape with full range of tones and sun included in shot	2,000,000 : 1
Bright landscape with full range of tones	1,000 : 1
Bride in white dress	100 : 1
Bright landscape with limited range of tones	60 : 1
Dull landscape	15 : 1
Aerial view	4 : 1
Misty or foggy view	2 : 1
All white pack on white background	Art Director's imagination!

Against this, one must set the theoretical range of tones which can be handled by the photographic process:–

	Range	
Black and white film	128 : 1	7 stops
Platinum print	100 : 1	6½ stops (expensive)
Bromide paper (soft/glossy)	50 : 1	5½ stops
Bromide paper (soft/matt)	20 : 1	4½ stops
Colour transparency film	16 : 1	4 stops
Colour print	8 : 1	3 stops
Bromide paper (very hard)	2 : 1	1 stop
Resin coated paper		No Comment!

Some of these figures are approximate, since very few cameras can be set to ⅓ stop increments.

This gives some idea of the problems we photographers have in trying to achieve any sort of ultimate result. Adams and Weston, in particular, took the art of printing as near as possible to the ultimate, by a combination of exposure, development and print dodging. Even these Masters would have no luck with modern transparency film, but could certainly get closer than most of us to any degree of perfection. Something somewhere has to give!

Gossen Profisix/Luna Pro SBC exposure meter.
Exposure time range 1/4000 sec to 8 hrs.
Measuring range at 100 ASA: EV −8 to 24.

SHOOTING BY AVAILABLE LIGHT

Whatever some sociologists may tell us, in some respects we are not equal. The ability to hold a camera still at low shutter speeds varies wildly from person to person. One's emotional state can also have a strong effect. Professional photographers develop a sense of calm when about to take a picture, no matter how exciting the circumstances. The techniques for avoiding camera shake range from the physiological to the mechanical. I knew one junoesque lady photographer who could repeatedly hand hold a one second exposure. The reason was that she used a Rolleiflex clutched to her considerable mass and gently squeezed the shutter release inwards. She told me that during the exposure she looked into the screen, lined up a point on the engraved grid and held it there until the buzzing (slow speed escapement gears operating) stopped. This technique would not work with a Hasselblad for obvious reasons!

Some single lens reflex cameras jump about alarmingly due to mirror action. On a few, any speed below 1/125 sec is dodgy in critical terms. Generally, the older generation of heavy SLR's are far easier to hold still, and rangefinder cameras can be effectively anything up to two stops faster than an SLR, simply because there is no mirror jumping about, and invariably these cameras have a light action shutter release. Most photographers need little excuse to play with their photographic toys, and in this respect there is a lot to be said for practising holding slow speeds with an empty camera, focusing and 'exposing' on incredibly boring subjects around the living room. It may annoy the hell out of the family,

what with all the buzzing and clicking going on – but then they can always turn up the T.V. There is a lovely story in an old Leica book of a photographer who practised his Leica technique in bed as a cure for insomnia. If you are a rangefinder freak, you may care to try taping a small mirror to the lens cap, then try to reflect the image of a bare light bulb on to a wall, but within the camera's field of view. You will be surprised how difficult it is to hold the camera still during a long exposure, though it will improve hand holding ability with practice.

EQUIPMENT AND GADGETS

Tripods are anathema to many available light photographers, who nevertheless will still resort to the use of ball and socket heads, G clamps and monopods as a half-way measure. Each has its own advantages. For outdoor use my preference is for a light-weight tripod. There are many who will say that this is no better than no tripod, but if used as a super monopod and weighted down, or braced by the photographer's body, surprisingly long exposures may be safely given, even in a wind, by shielding the camera and tripod with yourself. For indoor use I have an old but treasured German made G clamp, which has padded jaws, ball and socket head, three short screw-in legs and a vicious wood screw which is more suited to fence posts than other people's furniture. The whole slips easily into a pocket or corner of a gadget bag. I tend to regard long focal length lenses as fitting into the available light category simply because their invariably modest maximum apertures or physical length make

Minolta Auto Meter III exposure meter with liquid crystal direct readout. Exposure time range 1/2000 sec to 30 min. Measuring range at 100 ASA: EV −2 to 19.5 for incident light.

them a prime candidate for camera shake at anything less than optimum conditions. The use of a heavy tripod is preferable, though a monopod or bean bag is useful. In the absence of any mechanical aids, it is possible to use another person's shoulder as a steadying 'device', or a rolled up jacket on a car's roof, or hold the camera firmly down on a suitable surface. I have given one minute exposures this way. Be careful not to exert too much pressure on some compact SLR's which have plastic top — housings.

There are (and have been since pre-war) rifle stocks for fitting long focus lenses to various cameras. The theory, borne out in practice, is that this gives steadier exposures. But be warned. Some years ago, I hired a 600mm Novoflex rifle stock outfit in order to illustrate an article for a motor magazine. I positioned myself on a motorway bridge which was ideal for my purpose, sat down on a fishing stool and waited for suitable cars to come into view. What I did not know until later was that British Prime Minister Edward Heath was on his way to see his Mum and Dad further down the motorway, and that from the road I looked like a potential assassin. After two patrolmen and a carload of police had finished getting heavy with me, I abandoned my session. A friend of mine was not so lucky. Using a similar outfit in Tokyo, he was beaten up before anyone realised he was using a camera not a gun. Apparently there had been an assassination attempt on a government minister the day before and the police were still somewhat twitchy.

Movement is a complicating factor that makes ballet one of the more photographically demanding forms of theatre. Fast films are essential if you are to give yourself a chance of freezing motion under the relatively low levels of light. Wide-aperture lenses are obviously a boon, but it is important that you ensure depth-of-field is adequate for the shot you have in mind, and select shutter speed accordingly. A line of dancers will require different treatment from a ballerina's virtuoso piece. Remember also that lighting is likely to change scene by scene, both in colour and intensity, and hence keep a check on your meter readings. Do not be disappointed if you are unable to freeze all movement, blur can be creative.

SHOOTING BY AVAILABLE LIGHT

Gossen Lunasix III/Luna Pro exposure meter.
Exposure time range 1/4000 sec to 8 hrs.
Measuring range at 100 ASA: EV −8 to 24.

Short cable releases are a good way to transmit camera shake. This also goes for the heavily clad variety unless they are over twelve inches long. A good compromise is an air release which can be cut to any suitable length. These usually have a pipe connector about two feet from the bulb for just this reason. The compact bulb release is also useful for taking available light photos of yourself, or yourself and another. Under these circumstances a remote lead to a motor drive saves getting up to wind on and allows one to ham it up in front of one's own camera. Even full length shots are possible if the cable is held 'out of shot'. A bulb release can be foot operated. Self timers perform the same function when perhaps your picture requires a fore-ground figure. I have often used this technique when shooting boy, girl and car against a sunset type of shot.

Perhaps here a word about quietness. Rangefinder cameras such as the Leica have a big advantage, though many electron-ically controlled shutter SLR's are less noticeable at shutter speeds of $\frac{1}{8}$ sec and down due to lack of gear noise. There is a way of making your SLR almost as quiet as anything around, assuming your camera has a mirror lock-up facility. The trick is to use a Leica (or similar) optical viewfinder in the reflex camera's accessory shoe. After focusing, activate the mirror lock-up mechanism and look through the optical finder for framing. Few (if any) photographers can hold a reflex steady for longer than $\frac{1}{15}$ sec. This is partly psychological as staring through a black viewfinder window after the mirror has gone up is disconcerting, and without any reference point, camera shake is more than likely. Another tip for those of you with mechanically controlled speeds, is to make the exposure reading one second, but set the camera to B and use an oversized lenscap or piece of black card to control exposure time. Most people can guess one second accurately enough whether they count in hippopotami, potatoes or whatever.

I have used this trick when taking pictures in a quiet moment at a wedding or classical music concert. If your timing is good it is unlikely that there will be subject movement at an exposure of this length. Many experienced sports photographers learn the trick of slowing down time. This may sound like pure science fiction, but it is science fact. With enough absolute concentration the movements of say a high jump athlete, will slow down to a slow motion 'action replay,' enabling the shutter release to be pressed at the precise moment.

Reverting briefly to wedding photography: there are certain 'no no's' which apply to virtually any ceremony anywhere in the world. These are – not in any particular order – noisy cameras, flash, motor drives and tripods. Even T.V. crews, who get away with murder most of the time, have to keep a low profile with any religious ceremony, otherwise they do not get a chance of ever coming back. The same applies to you.

In view of the limited sensitivity of most in-camera exposure meters, a hand-held model designed to cope with low light levels is a useful investment for the night photographer. **Facing page top:** Car head and tail light streaks are evidence of a long exposure in this shot of the Severn Bridge. Tungsten balanced film was used, and this was responsible for the somewhat blue appearance of the scene. **Bottom:** Although the use of a tripod or some other improvised means of camera support is to be recommended for night shots, many scenes are deceptively bright, and can readily be photographed hand-held. Daylight films can be used uncorrected, as the resultant yellow cast is frequently considered acceptable. **Above left:** The intense light of a low, setting sun can flatten the appearance of your subject; if possible, move around to obtain the most pleasing modelling.

Copal Sekonic L398 selenium cell exposure meter.
Exposure time range 1/2000 sec to 60 sec.
Measuring range at 100 ASA: EV 4 to 17
for incident light.

BREAKING RULES

Rules may be made to be broken, or so we are told, but the photographer who knows the rules is able to break them to greater effect. He or she will not break the rules for the sake of breaking them, or out of ignorance, but because they know what they want. Too many young photographers are taught today that any image produced is valid providing that several pages of words are produced to justify the print or transparency. I hope that none of you will follow this line of thought, but that like a professional photographer, you will try to produce something out of nothing rather than not try to take a picture and perhaps later wish you had.

Having gone on at some length about not moving the camera during exposure, there are times when this can be most effective, even though your nearest and dearest will ask why your image is not as clear as usual. Perhaps the greatest exponents of deliberate movement have been America's George Silk, formerly of LIFE magazine, and England's Gerry Cranham. George went the whole gamut from long exposures to streak cameras, whilst Gerry homed in on wide angle long exposures from close distances before discovering zooming during exposure. I do not suggest that the family Pentax or Nikon should go to Marty Forschter for modification into a streak camera, for similar results can be obtained from the budget priced Cokin filter system, albeit with a fair degree of luck involved. The prime requirement of this kind of photograph is a dull day or a slow film speed or both. If you are stuck with a half-used high speed film in the camera, then use a gelatin neutral density filter in a proprietary holder to reduce the exposure to a useful level. Dependent upon the speed of your subject the shutter speed will vary from about $\frac{1}{15}$ to a full second. Don't be afraid to blow half a roll of film to learn this technique. The chances are that second time round you will hit it

in two or three frames. The same technique applies to zooming during exposure, with a couple of differences. Firstly, with a zoom lens, the camera is best mounted on a tripod unless you want 'steps' in your speed lines. Secondly, it is better not to start zooming until a third of the exposure has lapsed, or the subject is unlikely to 'read.'

It is preferable to zoom from a wide setting to a long setting with a stationary subject, though try a couple of frames the other way for the experience. You may prefer the effect. If you do not own a zoom lens, do not despair. Use your normal lens. Place the subject in the centre of the viewfinder to a size of one third the area. Tape a pencil firmly to the focusing mount to give leverage. After one third of the exposure has elapsed, wind the focus towards its nearest setting by moving the pencil. A firm tripod is essential for this one. This technique can even be used with a large format camera. In the case of a monorail, slide or wind the back to achieve the effect. Exposure time on large format is easier if in the one to three seconds area. You also will have the advantage of being able to 'play' on Polaroid before shooting for real.

All exposure meters can be fooled into giving a false reading, given that there is enough of a very dark or very light area in the subject. In available light pictures this can work for you or against you. Within our genre of pictures, under exposure is more often used to create mood. Try anything up to two stops less in addition to your metered exposure and then decide which you prefer. Caucasian skin will certainly stand a good stop under exposure, resulting in the background being toned down. A dull or colourless landscape can be improved by under exposure and the addition of a warming filter like an 81 series, or make it even colder and more forbidding by using an 82 series filter. Remember that the filter factor still has to be taken into account. Snow scenes at night can often be bettered by judicious under

*The good photographer is always awake to the possibilities of improving the shot. Although the gallery on the **facing page** was well illuminated by natural light, the opportunity of adding extra impact by turning on the lights was not lost. **Left and above:** A wide angle lens will achieve a given depth of field at a wider aperture than a longer objective, allowing faster shutter speed to be used to freeze movement.*

BREAKING RULES

exposure, particularly when the foreground is dark. A light source in shot can be one reason for going to over exposure since it can also fool your meter. These comments only apply to colour transparency films. With a colour negative film always go for correct (or over) exposure. Change of mood can be undertaken in the printing. The same goes for black and white work, where you also have the advantage of contrast control to give the effect you are after. Multiple exposures can be used creatively in available light photography. The accepted technique of multiple exposures of firework displays and lightning at night, is well known, though exposure determination has to be largely by guesswork.

As part of a recent assignment, I was asked to photograph a corner of a house at night, with only one window lit and the moon coming over a chimney . . . "And by the way, we want the trannies tomorrow." Since my own house fitted the layout and the forecast was for a clear night it all seemed O.K. It was soon obvious that the moon's path did not come over my roof. I shot the house from my front garden with a wide angle lens, and then going round to the back, double exposed the moon with a long tele lens, under exposing from meter by two stops to make the moon appear more yellow. I have often double exposed the sun – sometimes using a crosstar, to enliven a dull shot, but this was my first use of the moon in this way.

Flash (like a tripod) is often eschewed by available light photographers, but in my estimation, if it was acceptable to LIFE and PICTURE POST, then it is OK by me. Quite often you will find that there is simply not enough light around to produce anything but a silhouette of a subject. Back in the late nineteen forties, Kurt Hutton had a very low power electronic flash made for just this situation. The flash tube was used under a handkerchief to soften the light. Today there are dirt cheap tiny electronic flash units available which can be used for this purpose. If one of these tiny flash units is too powerful on your subject, bounce the light from a wall or ceiling, or tape a folded tissue over the tube. Most can be quickly reduced to give an f1.4 or f2 exposure even with fast film. If your electronic flash is an automatic unit, diffuse it (a single tissue cuts output by about one stop) or set the film speed indicator on the flash to a higher setting than the film in the camera. Dedicated flash units are mostly out since they electronically alter your shutter speed, but check yours. I have often used small flashguns in nightclubs which were too dark for photography. One would be placed above camera with a coloured gel over the tube, and an assistant would hold another – also gel covered – pointing towards the camera but some distance away. The technique was for me to fire my flash plus a time exposure for the house lights to record. As soon as my flash went off, my assistant fired his unit. The subjects were asked to stay still for the duration of the exposure. A similar situation occurred in one of those ultra violet lit discos of some years ago. With the cooperation of the MC and the band, the clients were encouraged to play at 'statues' at a signal, enabling me to give a time exposure. After a couple of takes, I realised that I was only getting a picture of white shirts and dresses. The faces could not be seen. Fortunately, I had my small flash and a blue gel with me: this lit the figures nearest to camera, the time exposure recording the glowing garments out of flash range.

Mention should be made of colour temperature, when dealing with some available light subjects. Theoretically, a black and white film used in artificial light loses speed for reasons of colour sensitivity. In practice, the latitude of the film will cover this loss when working with a small format emulsion. Sheet film users will invariably add a stop more exposure. Colour films do not display this tendency to the same degree. Tungsten balanced

Even, well diffused natural or artificial light is ideal in photographing interiors. Harsh shadows and hot-spots should be avoided, although reflections can be used to add depth and interest to shiny surfaces. Unwanted reflections can be removed with a polarising filter at the expense of film speed, or by careful positioning of the camera. Walls should, wherever possible, remain vertical; a close inspection of the viewfinder image, will avoid giving them an unnatural lean. **Right:** *Careful control of exposure enabled the photographer to show full detail of the foreground pillar carvings, without burning-out the parts illuminated by direct sunlight.*

BREAKING RULES

Train your eye to observe the effects of light on shape and colour, and develop your exposure techniques rather than relying on automation.

film is very tolerant of variations in light source colour temperature, coping admirably with domestic lighting or even car headlights and torchlight to a pleasing degree.

Using daylight balanced film in artificial light is acceptable to most of us who will accept warmth in an image. So if you only have a daylight film in your camera, and wish to take an artificial light picture, have a go rather than be purist about the matter. Professionals frequently use daylight film deliberately in this fashion in order to enhance the warmth of, say, a restaurant or bar interior. If you must correct, then use an 80B filter, but remember that there is a one stop loss of light, and if using an SLR that you will be viewing a one stop dimmer and bluer image.

Colour photography under fluorescent tubes gives a characteristic nasty yellow-green cast, which is particularly unflattering to flesh tones. This can be corrected to an acceptable standard with a magenta filter. Kodak issue a very comprehensive list of filter and exposure compensation for a variety of films and makes of tube. This is fine for professional photographers or those of you who consistently take photographs in the home or office, where it is possible to go up a ladder and find out which tube you are dealing with. In practice, use daylight film and a Kodak Wratten CC30M (magenta) gelatin filter which needs an exposure increase of ⅔rds of a stop. At worst, you will find that this correction filter will turn a yellow-green cast into brown, which most people find tolerable.

When using colour negative films, it is better to try and match filtration between light source and film. This may seem a hassle, but there is a technical condition called 'crossed curves', which can make a negative almost impossible to print to any pleasing degree. Even going halfway on filtration will help the

Vivitar 130LX exposure meter with liquid crystal scene brightness readout. Exposure time range 1/4000 sec to 8 hrs. Measuring range at 100 ASA: EV −2 to 19.

colour lab. In other words, when taking pictures of an artificially lit subject on daylight balanced film, and you do not have an 80B correction filter, then use ANY other blue filter such as a 'cc' blue, 82 or b/w 'half-watt', to give yourself – or the colour lab, at least a chance.

As you may have gathered, I am a great gelatin filter fan. With their modest cost and small physical dimensions it is possible to own a wide range. With care and the use of a proper holder, they can last a long time. I have gels which are twenty years old and still usable. One further advantage is that the three inch square filters can be used on a wide range of lenses, including most of my 5 x 4″ optics.

Reflectors are a useful way of helping available light photography, in a manner more acceptable to the purists than the use of fill-in flash. Though invariably restricted to domestic or studio conditions for reasons of bulk, there are now commercially available folding reflectors, (also in silver and gold), for those who do not wish to travel light. In the home, a spare piece of white painted fibreboard, polystyrene foam or an old sheet can be pressed into service to lighten shadow areas. Dimensions should be in the order of 4 feet square. Professional studios use 8 feet x 4 feet reflectors, several of which used together are enough to cope with a roomset. The reflector has the advantage that one can see its effect, which is not the case with fill-in flash.

SIMULATING AVAILABLE LIGHT

Simulation of available light can be as much a necessity for the amateur as the professional. This can happen whilst touring. A seascape presents itself. The sun is sparkling on the water which surrounds a dramatic rock formation – it would make a beautiful shot at sunset or by moonlight. Unfortunately you do not have the time to wait this long. The answer is to use a filter and under expose. For 'sunset' use an orange or 85B filter and cut

the exposure reading by three and four stops; do not allow for filter factor. For 'moonlight' use an 80B filter, or similar, at the same cut in exposure. A further sophistication is to use, additionally, a graduated filter to darken the top of the shot further. It is also possible to add a double exposed sun – with a 'crosstar' or diffraction grating, or to add a 'moon' by double exposing the sun, again through the blue filter. A medium to strong fog filter in combination with an 82 series blue filter can transform a subject into appearing more ethereal than reality. Avoid lighting conditions with long shadows for this one, and allow for filter factors.

For simulating available light indoors, one of the oldest dodges is to replace the bulb of a domestic standard lamp with a photoflood, which will raise the light level considerably without destroying the effect. A word of warning. Do not use this trick in a close fitting lampshade – particularly somebody else's. A photoflood gives approximately 800 watts of light with corresponding heat output!

One of my favourites is to use a door as a large light source, usually when a full length figure needs to be photographed on location. It is as simple as hanging a three foot wide roll of tracing paper over the open door frame and lighting from outside the room with a photoflood in a simple cheap reflector. Although flash can be used this way the results are uncertain unless a modelling lamp is part of the unit. There is also the matter of voltage drop on the sync. lead required. I have several times lit small interiors this way, by putting tracing paper over a window, and having my floodlight in the garden. In either case, the 'light source' should be out of shot, and the photoflood not less than three to four feet from the floor and several feet back from the tracing paper to avoid hot-spotting. The effect is similar to that produced by the giant electronic flash heads in the larger professional photographic studios.

POP

SUBJECTS POP

Pop music has become the opiate of the young masses, whether they stem from Moscow (Idaho) or Moscow (Russia). If my assistants are typical – which they probably are – then recording the antics of various hirsute anarchists is all part of life's revolutionary process. The violence of 'heavy metal' music is synonymous with the violence of the lighting effects. Rapid changes of colour, as well as pace, makes an automatic camera a virtual necessity. Match needle metering is almost useless without a clip-on illuminator and 'traffic light' LED's not much better.

Pop concert lighting levels tend to be low, although in a dark environment this does not appear to be so. Remember that T.T.L. meters will average what they see, so that the brightly lit pop idol gyrating against a darker background will end up over exposed. Likewise, since orange and red lights are part of the visual experience, this will throw the camera's meter – so, unless you have an automatic with an 'against the light' button, allow for another one or two stops more exposure. A spot metering facility can help – particularly if used during announcements – to give a starting point for exposure. If shooting in colour, then use a tungsten balanced film and be prepared to 'push' by two or three stops. Shutter speed should be short enough to stop frenetic movement – unless you happen to like blur. Use the fastest lenses you own. Zooms are usually a stop too slow for colour, unless the film is pushed to an insane ASA rating. Daylight balanced colour film gives such a warm subject rendering that most pop fans like the result.

If outrageous characters, frenzied expressions and a sprinkling of sex are what your photography lack, then go to a pop concert. But, be warned, sound levels and hysteria may run dangerously high, so unless you are an initiate, protect your eardrums and equipment. Select the fastest shutter speeds if you want to stop the constant movement, or use automatic cameras at full aperture. Automation will help you cope with constantly varying levels of light.

Pentax MEF aperture-priority automatic 35mm SLR camera with full manual override, fitted with 35-70mm f2.8 zoom auto-focus lens.

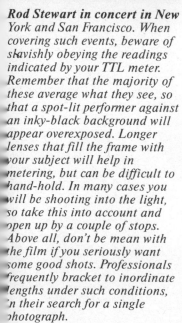

Rod Stewart in concert in New York and San Francisco. When covering such events, beware of slavishly obeying the readings indicated by your TTL meter. Remember that the majority of these average what they see, so that a spot-lit performer against an inky-black background will appear overexposed. Longer lenses that fill the frame with your subject will help in metering, but can be difficult to hand-hold. In many cases you will be shooting into the light, so take this into account and open up by a couple of stops. Above all, don't be mean with the film if you seriously want some good shots. Professionals frequently bracket to inordinate lengths under such conditions, in their search for a single photograph.

Zeiss 110mm f2 Planar lens for Hasselblad 2000 FC.

Professional photographers in the music business sometimes use the bracket and motor technique. This means setting a shutter speed of 1/250 sec, setting the motor drive going and winding the aperture scale backwards and forwards until the cassette is finished. Film is usually rated in the 800-1600 ASA range. Often a whole roll is treated as a 'clip' test. At some of the larger concerts, photography is forbidden, so check this out before you go. When seats are allocated, stay put. The big guys with broken noses who keep order for the promoters find wandering photographers a soft touch. Dads are advised to attend in disguise, take ear plugs for comfort, and a small torch to see what the hell you are doing. Carry the Nikax in an old khaki bag to deter the light-fingered. Above all, do not be disappointed with the results of your first attempt. Professionals use lots of film – they have to deliver the goods – and anyway the Record Company pays for it.

Smuggling your camera into a concert is a sure way of being asked to leave prematurely. Be certain to obtain written permission well in advance and choose a position where your activities will not annoy members of the audience. Tripods are definitely out, so avoid using lenses that you cannot hand-hold with confidence. It is well worth developing your own steadying techniques for just such occasions. Consider using a lens hood; with lights coming from different directions you are risking a degraded image due to flare.

THEATRE, FILMS, T.V., CIRCUS ETC.

THEATRE, FILMS, T.V., CIRCUS ETC.

Techniques for available light photography in theatres, film/T.V. studios and circuses are much the same as for a pop concert – which is after all only a modern version of opera. But there are some exceptions, so let's start with the general ones. Letting off flashes or using a motor at a pop concert will not matter – if you were to let off a cannon it would probably be assumed to be part of the act. Using the same machinery in other places will have you escorted (as distinct from being thrown) from the premises. On the one hand people pay for noise, on the other it can ruin their enjoyment or destroy the concentration of artist and technician alike. For this reason photography is forbidden at many big events, although there are likely to be fewer, if any, restrictions at country or community venues.

Much as we love photography, we must realise that even these functions are not put on for the benefit of camera enthusiasts, so unless you wish to louse it up for the next guy, keep a low profile. Rangefinder cameras which 'click' during quiet moments are just as annoying to others as SLR's which 'kerlop', so choose your moment carefully. It is a fact that certain film and T.V. studios in England will not allow photographers to use any camera but the rangefinder Leica. The days of shooting mute and dubbing afterwards are rapidly disappearing from the film business and have never been part of theatre or live T.V. It is no coincidence that sound deadening 'blimps' are now an optional (albeit expensive) accessory available from all the better camera makers. 'Long' shots showing the whole stage, arena or graphic paraphernalia of film/T.V. sets can be just as

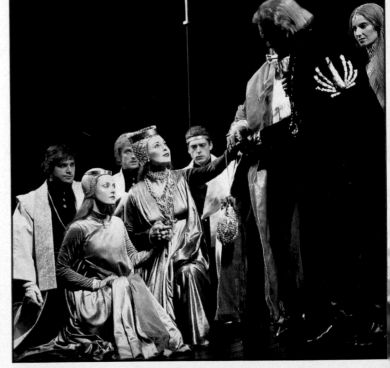

Technically, the serious theatre production differs little from the other types of stage show as far as the photographer is concerned. Artistically, depending on your tastes, the gap can be considerable. Here, however, you will benefit by concentrating on the expressive abilities of the actors – their faces as well as the gestures. Ideally, you will need to get up close, failing this you must resort to longer lenses, but, unless you have a particularly fast example, this will cost you around a stop in shutter speed.

Olympus OM 10 aperture-priority automatic 35mm SLR camera, fitted with 180mm f2.8 telephoto lens.

THEATRE, FILMS, T.V., CIRCUS ETC.

effective as close ups. Invariably, permission to take photographs is more likely to be obtained if one is prepared to work from outside the audience or technicians' area. Indeed, when my wife was on T.V., I obtained the 'close-ups' from a monitor in the control room. These, together with the wide angle and medium telephoto shots of the studio, gave us a more complete record of the event than was otherwise possible.

Theatre, ballet and opera can often be photographed better in close up during dress rehearsal. Again, permission is more likely to be granted, and access to vantage points, not available during the show, can be arranged. Even use of the Royal Box has been known to be possible. Most managements like to be rewarded by pictures. If you promise some, then keep your word and deliver same. Even if it is only a set of duplicate transparencies, do not leave it until too long after the event. People have short memories and the next time you want facilities they will remember the prompt photographer not the tardy one. It is not unusual for local theatre managements to commission photography at a later date, or at least trade pictures with free seats for the family.

Photography of classical music concerts fits into the same pattern, except that during rehearsals the artistes are unlikely to be wearing tuxedos or evening dress. Yet I find it charming to get a picture of a famous conductor or musician wearing a T-shirt and jeans. After all it does not affect their musical performance or standing. The same embargoes of no flash, motor drive, or shooting during quiet passages applies whether at rehearsal or concert. Fast film and fast lenses are vital if shutter speed is to be high enough to stop hand movements. I, for one, don't mind a bit of blurred polonaise or pizzicato for effect.

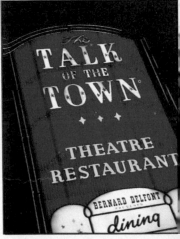

Facing page: Slow lenses may not be ideal for available light photography, but this does not make them useless. Many films can be uprated to give, in effect, several stops increase to the aperture of your lens. With transparency films, however, uprating leads to an increase in contrast. **This page:** Circus photography need not be restricted to the acts themselves. Look around at the expressions of fear and joy on the faces of the audience, observe the performers off-stage, the animals and the characters whose lives revolve around the big top.

THEATRE, FILMS, T.V., CIRCUS ETC.

Leica M4-P 35mm coupled rangefinder camera, fitted with 50mm fl Noctilux lens.

There can be no doubt that certain activities are inherently photogenic and ballet, with its graceful moves, balanced poses and the incredible agility of the dancers, is probably the most visually attractive of the performing arts. Ballet combines the appeal of both stage and figure photography, with highly trained and disciplined performers, who instinctively assume superb poses. As with sports photography, an understanding of the art, and even a knowledge of the particular drama being enacted, can be used to advantage in anticipating the various moves. Some poses are of course held for protracted periods, and it is worth waiting for these as they are invariably supremely graceful and also easier to capture.

Practice or rehearsal sessions are the only time that the amateur photographer is likely to be allowed access with his camera. This, however, can be used to advantage as, apart from the obvious benefit of being able to select a suitable vantage point, it will probably mean having a plain rather than photographically distracting theatrical backdrop. In addition, individuals. or pairs of dancers are often a more pleasing subject than a stage-full of whirling tutus.

THEATRE, FILMS, T.V., CIRCUS ETC.

It the circus visits town, then get as near the ring as allowed. Watch out for clowns with buckets of water. The audience will think a wet photographer is hilariously funny. Cameras do not have the same sense of humour. Use a long lens to record the expressions of the kids round the ring. These often make far better shots than fifteen people upside down on a horse's back.

Some circuses run daylight performances. The light coming through a traditional canvas tent tends to be somewhat yellow or brown. If shooting colour film, then use a blue filter like Wratten CC 10B to compensate for this colour cast. It will only cut exposure by one third of a stop, which in practice need not be allowed for. I have been to small circuses which used sodium lighting at night. This is virtually impossible to filter back and retain any respectable film speed. A Wratten CC 30M or CC 50M filter is a compromise but allow for two thirds or one stop respectively exposure increase. It is frankly better to shoot in black and white, where filtration is unnecessary. To complete a set of pictures, take shots around the circus outside the big top. Circus folk are friendly, and unlikely to raise objections, unless you do something stupid or get in the way.

Pentax ME Super aperture-priority automatic 35mm SLR camera with full manual override, fitted with 200mm f2.5 telephoto lens.

Silence during TV and film recording sessions is an absolute requirement. Professionals who frequently undertake on-set photography invest in sound-absorbing 'blimps,' or quiet rangefinder cameras of the Leica type. Even with these precautions, it is essential to avoid tripping the shutter at a quiet moment, when the slightest click may distract.

SPORT

SPORT

Most of the world is sports mad, so one can safely assume that possibly 90% of photographers also share this interest. At a quick count, there are something like fifty major areas of sporting activity, ranging from up-market recreations like hang gliding, to the international prestige stakes of athletics and tennis. To these one can add the health orientated pursuits such as marathons, cycling and even jogging! There are also the 'mind over machine' peripherals of motor and motor cycle racing etc., which have yet to be accepted alongside shooting and sailing by Olympic committees.

To be successful at any branch of sports photography, it is necessary to have at least some knowledge of the subject. Failing this, there is no substitute for practice. Photographers, being natural voyeurs, need not even use a camera, though if giving in to temptation, then waste a roll of black and white film practising. It is not necessary to print the results, it is cheaper than colour and shows you where you went wrong – ready for the next time. Apart, perhaps, from learning some of the finer points of the subject, the exercise will teach you anticipation. This is very important if you use a single lens reflex camera. Due to the delay between the mirror going up and the shutter operating, it is all too easy to get the subject disappearing out of frame, when you

were hoping to picture the peak moment. It is difficult psychologically, to press the shutter release before the subject is nicely centred in frame, but this must be learned. Rangefinder camera fans do not have this problem, nor do twin lens reflex users. Some rollfilm SLR's like the Hasselblad, have mirror lock-up facility and an accessory framefinder for all focal lengths and formats. The framefinder does have the advantage of letting the photographer know what is happening outside the field of view. Furthermore the image is life-sized. It can be very dangerous to view, say, a racing car out of control through an optical viewfinder. Everything seems so far away until too late. Folding framefinders for 35mm SLR's are now available from Japanese and German makers.

Shutter speeds for sports work should be high. Limbs mostly move faster than bodies and can need 1/1000 sec to freeze the action. Fortunately, most photographers do not object to some limb blur. Under poor lighting conditions it is often possible to pan with the subject, thereby allowing shutter speeds down to 1/30 sec – which will still allow a recognisable subject in the final photograph. Indeed, this can be a very dramatic way to convey an impression of speed.

The shutter speed necessary to stop movement varies with the direction of the subject relative to the camera. Head on motion will stand a longer shutter speed than across the camera.

Nikon FE aperture-priority automatic 35mm SLR
camera with full manual override,
fitted with 85mm f1.4 long-focus lens.

The ratio of shutter speeds is about 4 to 1. Diagonal movement towards the camera comes halfway between these two. With all sports work, the ability to focus fast and accurately is important, or so we are told. Certainly, it is preferable that all your lenses should focus in the same direction, whether clockwise or anti-clockwise. This becomes important when using a motor drive on 'continuous', and 'pulling focus' as the subject comes towards camera. With a lot of practice, it is possible to emulate the movie boys by 'pulling focus' and zooming from longest to shortest focal length simultaneously. A tripod can help with this technique. Novoflex still make a 'squeeze focus' pistol grip for their 400mm and 600mm lenses. This can be set for infinity or a closer distance. As the subject approaches camera, the pistol grip trigger

is released. Depending upon how fast or slowly the trigger is let out, the spring loaded focusing will move towards its closest setting, thus pulling focus with a high degree of accuracy. Most sports photographers will focus at a predetermined setting, releasing the shutter when the subject reaches this point. Old time press photographers used the same technique, often fitting a click stop device to the camera's focusing lever to give settings for, say, three, five, seven and ten yards. It was fascinating to watch them moving the focusing lever without taking their eyes off the play, as it moved nearer to, or further from, the camera. Later, when the TLR Rolleiflex became king in press work, a click stopped focusing knob was available for the same purpose. Leitz used to produce the Focorapid and Televit accessories for use with their long focus lenses. The former was for rapidly locating predetermined focusing settings, the latter a rapid focus device.

Zoom lenses with matching tele-extenders can be very useful when you are shooting from a fixed position. With sports work, the optical deficiencies of zoom lenses are seldom apparent, providing you keep the sun, or a strong light source, out of shot. Central definition is usually good enough to pull up a portion from the centre of a negative. Zooming in on a pre-determined focusing point needs more care with a 'one touch' lens. It is all too easy to add twist to zoom with a consequently out of focus image. For night sports' photography with zoom

The lighting at indoor sports *events is designed to simulate daylight, and whilst our eyes may accept this, colour films will not. The price, in speed, demanded by the use of* *correction filters is generally unacceptable for sports photography, so choose an appropriate film type and accept any slight casts.*

lenses push processing is essential. The modest maximum aperture often becomes even more modest at the longest focal length settings, which does not allow for quick shutter speeds.

Of all the sports events held at night, ice hockey and skating help the available light photographer most. The ice is a very good reflector of light, and in consequence can be a good stop brighter than, say, a field event held under similar lighting levels. When attending a sporting event, it is advisable to arrive early and

SPORT

make a pitch before the crowds arrive. Do check – with a compass if you like – that you will not be shooting into the light all day. Generally, it is better to face north rather than south for this reason. The same goes for a grandstand seat at any sporting event where photography is allowed.

When shooting under dull weather conditions on colour transparency material, it pays to allow for push processing of half to one stop. This not only helps with exposure at higher shutter speeds but produces a punchier transparency. Black and white workers can always print on a harder grade of paper. Colour negative enthusiasts may be able to get the lab to push half a stop – or do it themselves. In this case every little helps!

Bright weather conditions can produce another pictorial hazard: that is, too much depth of field. Football (or baseball) players are better separated from a sharp background of heads, stands and advertising bill-boards. I make a habit of using the camera's depth of field preview button before loading the film. Being a belt, braces and piece of string professional photographer, I carry film of three ASA speeds to any sports assignment. This allows me to control depth of field without the use of neutral density filters. Whilst the use of these is quite legitimate, they also reduce the intensity of my SLR's focusing screen by their marked factor, which can make life difficult on long focus, small aperture lenses. Sequence sports shots require a fast motor drive of 6 or 8 F.P.S. capability, a rapid winder is not quick enough for most subjects. Try timing a tennis serve or golf swing. Two or three frames is not enough. On the other hand a high jumper or pole vaulter has enough elapsed time to allow for a slower F.P.S. to give a good sequence. The same applies to an acrobatic high diver or some gymnastic exercises.

Water sports are a distinct hazard to cameras, particularly if pictures are taken from a boat. Salt spray is a quick way to say goodbye to an old friend – or a new one, come to that. There are various cheap plastic bag protectors available on the market, as well as expensive water orientated or sub-aqua camera housings. There also are inexpensive cameras made by Minolta and Fujica for wet picture taking conditions. These are more than adequate when the family photographic budget will not run to a Nikonos. The Fujica H.D. in particular would seem to be the answer to a boat owner/photographer's prayer.

Underwater photography really is in the available light category. 400 ASA film is a necessity, and colour photography, at even a few feet under the surface, requires CC 10 or 20 Red correction filters. Alternatively use a magenta biased colour film such as Fujicolor for halfway compensation. At depths below about six feet, a flash unit is necessary to avoid blue-green pictures. If you buy a camera or housing specifically for underwater photography, read the comprehensive instructions carefully. The refractive index of water does naughty things to estimated focusing distances – like shortening them by 25% for example.

I once worked for a travel company client, who asked for sub-aqua pictures for his brochure. As a non-swimmer, I dreaded this part of the assignment, but pride dictated that I had to go through with it. Fortunately a local enthusiast briefed me on the problems involved, and lent me a Nikonos complete with CC 20R filter. He also told me how to assess exposure by wrapping my Lunasix in a plastic bag – tested for water tightness – and held only just below the surface whilst the swimmer was 'in shot.' He also mentioned use of a glass bottomed boat, whose glass was so scratched as to be unusable for photography, but O.K. for metering. You've guessed it, I finally had to do it the hard way. Standing up to my chest in the warm Greek water, I waited until the 'model's' flippered feet disappeared below the surface, held

Minolta XD 7 multi-mode 35mm SLR camera, fitted with 35mm f1.8 wide-angle lens.

Low levels of ambient light *and slow films should not necessarily be considered a disability, as such a combination can be put to good creative use, even with the more demanding fast moving subjects. For the picture of the racing horse on the facing page, the photographer was obliged to use a slow shutter speed together with a panning action. This resulted in the characteristic streaking of the background and a speed-suggestive blur in the horse's legs and carriage wheels. The dark, unlit background serves to throw the rushing subject into strong relief.*

***Above: Effort and** concentration captured on the face of tennis star Bjorn Borg. A long focus lens was used at wide aperture to limit the depth of field and thus lift the subject from an otherwise distracting background. The narrow angle of view of the lens helped fill the frame with the subject and also enabled a more accurate TTL exposure reading to be made than would have been possible with a wider lens from the same viewpoint. **Above left:** A time exposure allowed for the firework bursts to be captured above the vast, illuminated Atlanta Stadium. In the absence of a tripod, walls or other solid objects can be used to steady the camera. **Left:** Houston Astrodome during a baseball game. A wide-angle shot such as this will go well with a series of close-up action photos.*

Olympus OM 1n 35mm SLR camera with TTL metering, fitted with 55mm f1.2 standard lens.

Apart from following the action at any sporting event, look also at the lines of photographers – their equipment and techniques. Notice how they often operate from a crouching position – this is not for the sake of comfort. The action shot taken from a low angle is often more dramatic than would otherwise be the case. A waist-level finder can be useful for this. Consider pre-focusing on a set position and wait for the subjects to enter your viewfinder. Use depth-of-field to obscure unwanted backgrounds.

my breath, ducked under the water and pressed the button. After twenty exposures and getting half drowned, I called it a day. There are some clients one can do without! When the film was processed, I had 'managed' two adequate shots. Upon returning to London, my partner was not sympathetic. "You stupid ---," he said. "You could have done those shots in a swimming pool with an observation window." I was suitably chagrined. He was quite right. So if Junior wins his underwater swimming spurs, you know how to record the event in comfort and without having to buy a special camera. You can even use an automatic flashgun if camera and flash are held against the glass.

Reverting back to terrafirma for the finale, there are a few techniques for sports photography which may be of use. Once more we have the no no's of motors and flash for those events where a photographer can cause distraction or annoyance. In particular, Golf, Tennis, Gymnastics, Fencing and Pool spring to mind. Often a waist level viewfinder facility (2¼" square cameras specially) is useful. The low viewpoint can dramatise the athlete's stance or action, and furthermore is useful in avoiding a background of brick walls or other stadium detritus.

Sometimes one is nailed down to a fixed position, and has forgotten (or does not own) a sufficiently long focal length lens. Don't despair. Black and white workers can shoot the subject anyway and later make a sectional enlargement to 10 x 8". They can print half to one grade softer than normal, then copy the result. This allows for greater magnification than the enlarger column normally facilitates. An alternative is to use a good cine lens of 15 or 25mm focal length and enlarge a 110 sized section. The picture area selected must be central in the enlarger negative carrier. Rollfilm users can perform the same trick with a 35mm or 50mm enlarger lens. A fine grained original black/white negative helps. This technique is not suitable for colour negative work except in desperation. Colour transparencies are better duped or re-photographed from a screen. More of this later on. If it is your ambition to be an ace sports photographer, – how do you start?

The organisers of local events and matches are far more amenable to granting photographic facilities than their national counterparts. It helps to get at least freelance sanction from the local newspaper or magazine. It helps even more to appear at the event as their accredited photographer. Just as with press work, it is a matter of building a portfolio. Photograph kids' sporting fixtures and don't forget the human interest shots. If a sporting hero makes a charity appearance in your area, be sure to get your first celebrity picture. Maybe you know an archetypal sportsperson. Get them to do a photo-call for you. Try all those angles and gimmicks which cannot be taken for real. This is exactly what an advertising photographer would do. In his case, the final result could be to promote a toothpaste or laxative. You are promoting your friendly sportsperson and yourself.

NIGHT SCENES

NIGHT SCENES

Photography at night has always been a challenge to photographers. Perhaps Ansel Adams' superb "Moonrise over Hernandez" is the most famous, and at up to $70,000 a print (according to 'Modern Photography') so it should be. "Moonrise" is in fact not a night shot as such, but was taken at dusk. As a general rule, whether talking about black and white or colour, the best night shots are taken at dawn or dusk when there is still a semblance of light in the sky. This has two effects. Some foreground detail is retained, and in the case of colour film there is still some colour in the sky. The snag with working at dawn or dusk, is that day and night happen much faster than expected. Light levels change drastically within half an hour – less nearer the equator. Be prepared to work fast and bracket exposures. Assuming that the blandishments of bed are not overwhelming, it really is worth the effort. As usual, there are exceptions to this dictum. A long shot of a city or industrial plant from ground level, will retain an aura consisting of smog and street lights (particularly in winter), regardless of time of night and particularly when the sky is cloudy.

The choice of camera equipment for night photography is immaterial. It just depends upon your attitude to tripods. In a brightly lit city centre, even Kodachrome 25 allows for hand held exposures with an f1.4, or better still f1.2 lens. More depth of field or a slower lens dictates use of a faster film, or a tripod and cable release. Black and white film is not only faster for night photography, there is also the bonus of printing on different grades of bromide paper, to give a degree of contrast control. The possibility of using "ASA" ratings of up to 10,000 exists, if you don't mind postcard sized prints with horrendous grain and no shadow detail.

Black and white films are rated under daylight conditions – where there is a high proportion of blue light, so there is a loss of up to one stop in speed when used with redder tungsten lighting. In practice, a half stop push in processing will compensate for this, since a full stop extra exposure only accounts for 30% increase in negative density. Certainly with 400 ASA materials, there is sufficient exposure latitude to give a printable negative at ASA 200 or 800. Agfa Vario-XL and Ilford XPI have even more latitude.

Don't wait for complete *darkness before you set out to photograph the cityscape at night. All you are likely to get are vague outlines of buildings and a bewildering number of pin-pricks of light. Use the remaining light and colour in the sky to breathe some life into the picture. If you have the opportunity of using a high viewpoint, don't forget to experiment with lenses of different focal lengths.*

NIGHT SCENES

with daylight film, then use a Wratten 80A blue filter or similar. TTL metering should compensate without any adjustments being necessary. With other metering, halve film speed and don't forget to reset the ASA scale when the filter is taken off the camera. It is better not to push process with high contrast night scenes, though a one stop push will probably provide acceptable results, and a three stop push is possible before colour shift, contrast and grain get really objectionable. The 3M 640T emulsion should only be given a one stop maximum push. Type B film will give an intense blue sky when used at dusk.

Apart from a camera, small torch – to set controls – cable or air release and filters, there remains the question of supporting the camera. Whilst a heavy tripod is the ultimate, there are many times when this is inconvenient or just too much bother. As mentioned earlier in this book, I am a G clamp fan, but there are times when there is nothing to clamp it on at the chosen viewpoint. My late uncle left me a nine inch long, pre-war, flat tripod with a ball and socket head. This has accompanied me on my travels for the last fifteen years. Whilst in itself it could well be described as flimsy, when weighted down with small gadget bag it has got me out of trouble many times. It is imperative to use the mirror lock-up facility on my 35mm cameras or Hasselblads but even so – – –.

Fire and water react to a variation of shutter speed in a similar way. Flames can be made to appear as well defined tongues, or may simply disappear into a general blaze. 'Correct' exposure is subjective, and depends on the effect you wish to achieve. If the scene includes people you may decide to show them in outline, or you can paint them dramatically with the light from the flames. Think of the fire as a miniature sun, and calculate your effect from there.

Colour negatives do not take kindly to being pushed in C41 chemicals. In fact, many labs will not undertake this at all, particularly if they are expected to print the resulting negative! On the other hand, only Vericolor IIL is balanced for artificial light. It is rather slow at 100 ASA and is not available in 35mm form. Most of us will accept the warm rendering of daylight 400 ASA films exposed to artificial light. If not, an alternative is to use a Wratten 80A blue filter which effectively cuts film speed to 200 ASA, and takes most of the 'hotness' out of the print. There are also some rather naughty techniques for processing reversal colour materials in C41 colour negative chemicals. This will not be discussed in a later chapter!

Colour transparency films for night scenes should again be of the tungsten balanced type. If your camera is already loaded

Uncle's old faithful has now been augmented by a multi-sectioned tiny Japanese tripod. Depending upon how light I am travelling, I would hate to be without either. At a pinch, the Japanese mini tripod will even take my 5 x 4″ Linhof or Nagaoka, which is really its raison d'etre. I have removed its mini pan and tilt head, which is not up to the job. This has the result of making the tripod more rigid and compact. Finally, on the subject of tripods, a centre column is the biggest cause of camera shake: do not extend it unless you really have to.

Night scenes when lit by high intensity street lights and/or fluorescent tubes can cause colour temperature problems, when any degree of colour fidelity in the subject is desirable or necessary. Each type of light source requires different filtration. Even an expensive colour temperature meter cannot help here,

Leica R4 multi-mode automatic 35mm SLR camera fitted with 50mm f2 standard lens.

s most types of public utility lighting have what is called a iscontinuous spectrum, which cannot be measured accurately.

Whilst it is sometimes possible to make test shots with a ariety of filters, more usually it is a matter of compromise – nything rather than the invariably yellow-green result. I carry 'ratten CC 30 and CC 50 Magenta gels, as well as proprietary FL- /B glass filters. The exposure increases are ⅔rds and one stop

respectively. My Nikon and Leica R3 TTL systems compensate for this exposure factor without any trouble. Whilst I cannot answer for other untried makes, I would not expect anymore than ½ stop under-exposure. Black and white film is unaffected by fluorescents and the like, so needs no special consideration.

Window displays, bars, clubs and restaurants can be lit by tungsten spot lamps or domestic light bulbs. Daylight colour film will give a great subject warmth which can be appealing. For greater colour fidelity use a blue correction filter or tungsten balanced film. If in doubt shoot the subject with and without correction filter. One is bound to be more pleasing than the other, and you do then have a choice of colour rendering.

A lyricist once wrote, "By the light of the silvery moon." In fact, it is not silvery, though it can be a burned out white with over-exposure. As we now know (from astronauts' colour photos) the moon is shades of yellow/brown. I once read that "pictures taken by moonlight should be on daylight balanced film, because the moon is lit by direct sunlight." What this enthusiast failed to mention, is that the moon has a coloured surface and will reflect that colour. He was correct in his assumption that daylight balanced colour film should be used. But, to counteract this yellow/brown cast and to allow for reciprocity failure, (more on this later) Kodak recommend cyan and/or blue filter correction with their daylight balanced film.

Tungsten balanced film will over-correct towards blue – just like the cinema cliché of blue moonlight and under-exposure. Photography of the moon itself is not difficult. It is very bright – the same as a daylight exposure in fact. You will need a lens of at least 1000mm focal length to get a good sized image on 35mm format, when the moon is high in the sky. At horizon level, or a bit above, a 300 to 500mm lens will suffice, and exposures will be longer due to atmospheric conditions. In either case a heavy tripod is essential. Yes, it is possible to shoot hand held, but try keeping the damn thing accurately in frame! Atmospheric conditions affect exposure and definition. Slower colour films will give better results. Err on the side of under-exposure if in doubt, particularly since some TTL meters are not as centre-weighted as others.

Landscapes lit by moonlight are best taken near or at full moon – some photographers get quite excited at this time anyway. Keep the moon out of shot, (except when it is low in the sky), as it will move considerably during the necessary ten or fifteen second exposure. Moonlight on the sea looks terribly romantic and is virtually impossible to photograph. Even with the fastest film or lens, a shutter speed of around 1/60 sec is necessary to stop wave movement or the rocking of a boat. The effect can be simulated in daylight. Urban landscapes tend to be lit more strongly by street lights than by moonlight. I have seen some very effective cityscapes, with the moon double exposed into a gap between buildings.

Facing page top: This kaleidoscope of firework patterns was captured by opening the shutter and covering the lens between explosions, to avoid overexposing the illuminated buildings. **Bottom:** *A long exposure empties the Champs Elysées, recording only the ghostly light trails of passing cars.*

NIGHT SCENES

Facing page: Hong Kong Harbour by night. The two pictures were taken at the same time and from the same viewpoint, using tungsten and daylight balanced films, clearly demonstrating the effect obtainable from the two emulsions under identical conditions. *Above:* The lights of the Forth road bridge create torch-like reflections in the lapping waters below. The graceful outline of the structure is backed by an evening sky whose colour is mirrored in the water. *Top:* Ornamental fountains take on the look of steaming geysers when pictured using slow shutter speeds. At night, you may find you have no option.

Leica R4 multi-mode automatic 35mm SLR camera fitted with 135mm f2.8 telephoto lens.

NIGHT SCENES

Metering for moonlight photography is best achieved with a hand held exposure meter, such as the Gossen Lunasix, used in the incident mode. In-camera metering systems do not have enough low light capacity for this game. It is possible to take a reading off a piece of white paper or card, and then multiply the exposure by between sixteen and one hundred and twenty eight times – or four to seven stops, depending upon the amount of shadow detail you wish to record. If your camera is loaded with slow film and the meter's ASA dial set accordingly, you may not even get a reading. In this case, move the ASA setting to as high as it will go, take a reading and transpose to the correct setting. Finally, multiply by one of the factors mentioned. Don't forget to reset the ASA dial to normal.

This technique works for colour or black and white. Lights at night can be metered direct with a TTL system, though shadow detail is likely to be minimal. Open up two or three stops to get a compromise between colour in the lights and some shadow detail. Wet streets bounce more light about and will probably only need plus a half or plus one stop over meter reading. Again, both these adjustments can be made on the ASA dial or exposure compensation control when fitted to your camera.

Reciprocity failure is the inability of any black and white or colour film to cope with ultra short, or ultra long exposures, without some compensation being made to film speed. In the case of colour films there is also a shift in colour balance. As a guide, a 10 second exposure will need plus one to plus one and a half stops over meter. A 2 minute exposure may well need up to two and a half stops compensation. Colour balance shifts on colour film can be anything up to CC30 in strength – usually towards a yellow or green bias. Consult the maker of your favourite film if you intend to make long exposures consistently, or if a colour bias worries you.

A few last thoughts about night photography. Urban landscapes can be enlivened (to choice) with streaks from traffic headlights and tail lights. Composition freaks will tell you that these lead the eye into the picture. They do have a point. Before you start shooting for traffic streaks, time the passage of a vehicle entering and leaving your picture area, and adjust the exposure accordingly. Traffic lights need to be allowed for, or the streaks can 'disappear', as if the vehicles concerned were suddenly spirited away.

Long exposures in urban areas enable a photographer to 'lose' passers-by, who are not present for the total exposure time. This technique is often used by professional photographers for night shots of new buildings or shopping precincts.

There is a fun method of producing abstracts, to use up those last few frames. It requires a profusion of neon signs.

Use your TTL meter for a direct reading – without compensation. Stop down enough to give a one second (or longer) exposure. Fire the shutter, and wave the camera around in the direction of the neon signs. Passers-by may think you're mad, but you know what you are doing, at least after the first attempt! As an alternative, after a night session on Type B colour film – again with those few frames left on the cassette or roll – try some daylight exposures <u>without</u> a correction filter. The effect is quite different from using a blue filter on daylight stock, and adds yet another technique to your photographic armoury.

Using flash at night may be anathema to available light photographers. So often we have seen those sub-amateur optimists, who fire a flash equipped 'Instamatic' at an Oberammergau passion play or Madison Garden world championship fight. We smile condescendingly, or mutter four letter words, yet they can teach us something. A colleague of mine, taking a holiday in Spain, did just this. His inadvertent use

of flash plus time exposure produced a superb pink stuccoed frame for the night shot of the city beyond. Had he not used flash, the foreground interest would have been nil. Even after more years than one cares to remember as a professional photographer, one can still learn!

Two more tips, before moving on to the next subject. Firstly, if you have shot a whole roll of night shots in colour, it is better to have the roll returned UNCUT from the processors. Automatic slide mounting machinery – and its operator – cannot be blamed for not knowing where to crop your shots. Secondly, don't get mean about bracketing night shots when they are unrepeatable. After all, a few extra frames come cheap when measured against the total cost of a holiday.

The city at night assumes a totally different character that invites the attention of the photographer. Fine pictures are possible with the most modest equipment, as long as the camera permits long exposures. Tripod and cable release are of course useful accessories that will help avoid blurred shots. Due to the rather mixed nature of the light, no single film-type is likely to give a natural rendering and although tungsten film is considered the norm, you may find the colours from daylight film more pleasing.

REPORTAGE & PRESS

REPORTAGE AND PRESS

Press photography is more a test of resourcefulness than photographic skill. The old adage that "yesterday's news is no news" still generally applies. Of course, there are stories which run for several days, though more often than not, something else happens in this troubled world to make the new headlines. A personal 'for instance' will clarify this point.

Many years ago, whilst still a student, I happened to be walking along London's Oxford Street, when a double decker bus crashed spectacularly info a store front. Though I didn't know it at the time, several people were killed. I took a roll of film on my TLR Rolleiflex, both from street level and from a staircase window opposite the scene. I knew enough to take the undeveloped film straight to my chosen newspaper office. I suppose it took me half an hour of running and walking to reach

Above: For this wide-angle shot of a Cairo classroom, the meter was shielded from the light of the high window. ***Right and top right:*** *These scenes were exposed to show maximum shadow detail without burning-out the highlights or subject flesh tones. Incident light* metering gives the photographer complete control in such circumstances. ***Facing page top:*** *Exposure compensation was avoided to achieve impact and simplicity.* ***Bottom:*** *The Ceremony of the Holy Fire in Jerusalem's Holy Sepulchre.*

REPORTAGE & PRESS

Photographs can take on a historical significance earlier than one may imagine. The pace of change and improvement is constantly escalating; work methods change, whole industries vanish and buildings disappear with alarming regularity and speed. With this in mind, the camera can take on a new significance, and the photographer an attitude of increased interest and awareness in his surroundings. The benefit of hindsight is that it can teach us to look more closely at our world in the future. Shown on these pages is the world famous, but now relocated, Billingsgate Fish Market, London, where baskets full of crabs are being lowered into vats for boiling. There is a certain charm in the dilapidated state of the building and its primitive equipment, that cannot be found in the clinical efficiency of more modern premises. It is worth paying attention to smaller details in such photographic essays.

Leica R4 multi-mode automatic 35mm SLR camera fitted with 35mm f2 wide-angle lens.

Fleet Street. What I did not know was that another amateur photographer had taken a taxi! His pictures made the evening edition by a few minutes. Mine, though much better – according to the Picture Editor – were twenty minutes too late. There was, however, a sequel to this story. Now knowing the Picture Editor, I bombarded the poor man with lots of unsuitable material for the next few months, until he published a picture of a crashing racing car. The fee just about covered my costs from the circuit, but oh the glory!

Getting a scoop is not always a matter of luck. You can shorten the odds by always carrying a camera. The chances are that the day you leave it at home is when something happens. How often have you heard someone say "If only I'd had a camera." It may seem prudent always to carry an SLR and a wide angle and a telephoto and a motor drive etc., but this is not necessary. A pocket sized 35mm automatic with built in flash, plus a roll of 400 ASA black and white film, is all that is necessary and furthermore no effort to carry. After all, some famous scoops have been enlargements from amateur 8mm ciné frames. Press photographs are judged on newsworthiness and not by photographic criteria. It may be that no drama will ever cross your path; even so there will be other photographs you would not otherwise have had – dramatic sunsets, celebrities on the street, or the incongruous, like a pony and trap caught in a city traffic jam – which was taken by a friend of mine.

Newspapers and magazines use feature pictures too, as space fillers. Here you often have time to develop and print your own film. Don't wait until the film is finished. Open the camera back in the dark, carefully cut off the exposed frames and develop these. The remaining short length of film can be used for test shots, or put back in the camera. A reminder, stuck to the camera back, of the approximate number of frames left, is a good idea, particularly if the camera is not often used. For the same reason use only one type of film.

Taking press or reportage pictures locally at weekends is a good training ground as well as a way of building up a portfolio. Most of the time, no special permissions or police passes are necessary. I once took pictures at a Bank sports day. Looking at the contact sheets, the best shots were of amateur athletes doing it all wrong. I submitted these to the Bank's house magazine, together with the champions doing it all right. I was surprised that a whole page was devoted to the triers. I had expected some

REPORTAGE & PRESS

repercussions from the subjects, as nobody likes being made to look foolish. There were none. In fact I received several requests for prints. One man thought it was the funniest picture of himself he had ever seen – and framed it. I was subsequently commissioned by the Bank to shoot other events.

Once you have built up a portfolio, show it to the local papers. Often they only have a few photographers, and will be

Canon A-1 multi-mode automatic exposure 35mm SLR
camera. fitted with 85mm f1.2 long-focus lens.

happy to put you on the freelance list. They will not necessarily commission you, but will always look at what you submit. You must be serious about press work to go on a list. There is always the possibility that a phone call in the middle of the night will result in a wild goose chase. You have to reconcile the minimal expenses against the loss of sleep. Invariably, to turn down the request will shut the paper's door to you. It is not possible to pick and choose at this level. Excuses are seldom accepted. Don't worry about scooping the staff man. He may wish he had taken your shot, but can't be everywhere at once. Anyway he gets a regular salary. What he <u>will</u> object to, is if you follow him around. Find your own unusual angles and let the best picture win.

If shooting a disaster, remember that the general shot is more likely to be used; try to include a recognisable landmark. Close-ups of blood stained victims are best left to those with police passes. Getting in the way of the emergency services is asking for a busted camera or, worse still, head. This is particularly true during civil commotions. Talk your way into an upstairs vantage point. It may cost you, but what the heck!

Although this is a book about using available light, do not hesitate to use flash in press photography. A clear picture is more likely to be used than an artistic mood shot. Prints should be slightly harder than normal with a glossy surface. Resin coated papers, which wash and dry quickly, are fine for this purpose.

A nostalgia for fine workmanship and hand crafting has led to a resurgence of small, one-man industries that honour the time-worn traditions of specialist manufacture. These can make fascinating subjects for photography, but remember that these people have a living to make and, unless you are a customer, they cannot afford to devote much time to posing for photographers. The contemplative nature of many of the tasks lends itself particularly well to available light treatment. **Facing page top right:** *A particularly fitting subject; Fred Gandolfi puts the finishing touches to a hand-made wooden view camera – a hundred years after the founding of the firm by his father.* **Bottom left:** *Handloom weaving survives as a cottage industry in many parts of the world, the workshop and sales room often being one and the same.* **Bottom right:** *The village blacksmith still exists, but now his work is likely to be somewhat more diverse.* **Centre right:** *A French sabot maker fashions a pair of clogs, still worn in some parts of the country.* **Bottom:** *The pyrotechnic effects of a welder's torch always make for an interesting picture.*

Look at newspaper office window displays for guidance. Self adhesive paper stickers are useful for captioning resin coated papers, which smudge easily. Write up your caption label <u>before</u> it goes on the print to avoid printing through. Use capital letters for clarity. Caption sheets should also include your name, address and phone number. Small stickers bearing the same information can be stuck to undeveloped cassettes for obvious reasons, and are easily kept in a wallet ready for use.

Even if after a lot of effort, none of your pictures ever get published, the family will still have a good record for posterity, and you will have had some excitement in the process.

PEOPLE & PORTRAITS

PEOPLE AND PORTRAITS

Photography of people by available light is, and always has been, a prime subject for the camera. I would subdivide this into pictures taken with and without the permission of the subject. One's family and friends usually fall into the 'with' category, even though permission is tacit because of the relationship between photographer and subject. All of us have taken pictures unbeknown to the 'sitter'. It could be a shot of grandad dozing in a chair, with his spectacles falling from his nose, or the baby asleep in its cot, or the wife, en deshabille, making up her face. In each case, it is a fond moment to be captured for posterity and takes nothing from the subject. As photographers, we are necessarily voyeurs and opportunists. Once we realise this, we are less likely to give offence.

I once took a picture of my uncle – who was chronically ill, sitting with my father – who had broken a hip bone. The sunlight dappled through the trees at eventide, back lighting two old men sitting hunched over their walking sticks. I reacted automatically to the situation. Neither was aware of my presence. When my father saw the print he was horrified that I could portray him, and my uncle, of whom I was supposed to be fond, in this manner. Though I say it myself, the picture was good, but in very poor taste. I tore up the print and apologised to my father, but he was wary about being photographed from then on. Many years later, I

The attractive available light shot need not rely on the unusual view for its success. Everyday scenes, as shown **top and left,** owe their appeal as much to lighting as to subject matter. **Above:** The hookah smoker in a Cairo cafe is the type of shot a tourist should look out for. **Facing page top:** These pictures show the different effects obtained by using daylight (left) and tungsten films (right) under artificial light conditions. **Bottom left:** A wide angle lens is frequently the single choice of those wishing to travel light. **Right:** Dying crafts are always a fascinating subject.

Minolta XG-M aperture-priority automatic 35mm
SLR camera with full manual override,
fitted with 200mm f2.8 telephoto lens.

am still ashamed of that shot. It is not the way I care to remember either of them.

Perhaps the old maxim should now be qualified as "when photographing others, do unto them as you would have done unto you." Nowadays, there are far too many photographic exhibitions of murky pictures portraying unfortunate or under-privileged people, being produced by 'socially concerned' photographers. We all know of several who have made a name for themselves out of their 'social conscience'. Perhaps worse, this sort of photography is now part of many a photographic college's curriculum and, as such, actively encouraged. I honestly feel that this kind of photographic intrusion into other people's misery does nothing for the recipient of social injustice. A photographer would do much better to buy his subject a decent meal, or perhaps a bottle of better stuff, rather than expend rolls of film for a diploma. Even worse is the 'ego' photographer who is certain that his pictures will convince the great general public that 'something should be done'. It seldom is, but for political propaganda, such pictures can raise some votes, as both A. Hitler and Franklin D. discovered.

PEOPLE & PORTRAITS

Portraits by available light, and utilising a big window as the light source, can be taken at any time of the year. It is better that no direct sunlight falls upon the subject. If it does, then tape tracing paper, or net curtaining, over the window to diffuse the light. A big north facing window – as traditionally used by artists – is ideal. To place the subject sideways or three quarters towards the window will produce the so-called Rembrandt lighting. A portable projector screen can act as fill-in or white background. With ladies of a certain age, it is kinder to keep the window behind the camera, as softer lighting is more flattering. A good diffuser, such as Hasselblad's Softar 2, over the lens will help here as well. As with any other portraiture, keep the camera lens height slightly above the subject's eye level and use a longer focal length lens than the normal. If possible keep the shutter speed to 1/125 sec if hand holding. You can go down to 1/15 sec if using a tripod. The lens aperture should allow for five or six inches depth of field, to cover the distance between tip of nose and ears. Focus on the eyes. If you cannot get this depth of field, pull the camera back and get a smaller image in the frame. Alternatively let the subject's ears go out of focus. Children and babies can be photographed at a wider aperture than an adult,

If the natural female nude, as opposed to the overtly sexual glamour picture is what you are seeking, then daylight is the ideal medium. This isn't to say, however, that you should not manipulate it to your own ends. Indeed, the light can, and often must be reflected, diffused, re-directed and obscured if you are to achieve the effect you desire. Contre-jour is a technique beloved of many photographers of the nude, as shown here, and with good reason. It can enhance softness and emphasise curves, apart from which it seems to be the way that we expect to see the natural, relaxed and credible nude figure.

simply because they are smaller.

The subject should be seated in a low-backed chair – to save too much refocusing between frames – and with their shoulders at an angle to the camera. Most professional portrait photographers always use a tripod. The reason for this is that it is necessary to talk to the subject over the camera to get some rapport going, or to give instructions. Too many amateurs mumble away behind the camera and then wonder when their pictures look wooden. Medium format cameras have the enormous advantage of accepting Polaroid backs. Two or three black and white Polaroids provide a discussion point between subject and photographer. Colour Polaroids take too long to develop and are unnecessary unless colour content is an essential part of the photograph. Don't try to get the shot you are after on a few frames. Even professional models need half a dozen or so to warm up. As a guide, the best shot on a Hasselblad always seems to happen on frame 13, which is why professionals use roll one as the test film. Another technique to get the model going, is to blast off the first shots on 35mm, then switch to 2¼″ square. Part of successful portrait photography is knowing how to direct. This does not mean forcing your personality upon the sitter, though very occasionally this may be necessary. Good direction is more a matter of mutual understanding through gentle persuasion. The fashion photographer's patter, as immortalised in Antonioni's film "Blow-up":– "Great, great! I love it! Super! Yes, yes! Beautiful! Come on baby! Give it to me! Yes, yes!", and so on in the same orgasmic manner, would make most models laugh today. Perhaps the more naive still enjoy this mixture of cajolery, praise and flattery.

Being on the 'wrong' side of the camera occasionally is

Leica M4-P 35mm coupled rangefinder camera, fitted with 135mm f2.8 telephoto lens.

People at work, whether craftsmen or barmen, have always fascinated the photographer, and will no doubt continue to do so. The diversity of subject matter, method of treatment and interpretation make this a particularly rich area for exploration. You may decide to draw attention to the personality of the subject, to the particular skills of the job or to the surroundings within which he or she works. You have the choice of using either colour or black and white film to reinforce this interpretation; of exposing only for the highlights to get a more dramatic image; of selecting the lens to show what interests you. This is where your style is likely to emerge, and where your adaptability will be put to the test. No single technique can be applied to such a wide-ranging subject, where, amongst other things, light will be as varying, and perhaps variable, as the people's occupations. If you intend to shoot candid, unposed pictures it is worth considering fast film and a long lens, alternatively, a cramped workshop may mean that a wide-angle is required. It is as well to be aware of the various problems beforehand if you are to bring home the goods.

PEOPLE & PORTRAITS

good for the photographer's soul. Most of us – like doctors who make lousy patients – are not happy to be the subject. The very self-confident, or extrovert, find acting out a role easier, and, let's face it, portraiture does require a certain amount of facial animation. To smile to order, as distinct from to laugh, is not a matter of grinning uneasily. Actors learn to smile with their eyes as well, in order to be convincing. Most of us benefit from a drink before hamming it up in front of the camera. As a prelude to photography, this is also useful for getting to know a new subject. Find out his or her interests and be a good listener. This will help them relax and avoid the – "I hate having my picture taken. I'd rather go to the dentist" – syndrome, which does nothing for a photographer's self esteem – or social status!

Another form of available light portraiture which is far less formal, is the 'pictures of people at work' category. Providing you don't make an act of it and get in the way, very few people object to being portrayed at something they do well. This, of course, includes hobbies. Even if they are not expert there is always the let out of, "The painting wasn't finished," or "You should have seen the pot I threw last week," or "I was practising a difficult cantabile passage, which is why my face is screwed up."

If care with lighting is important in girl photography, then so also is the choice of setting. It is not much use arranging your model's pose with utmost care if you leave the props and surroundings to chance. If in doubt, settle on simplicity – after all, what is not there cannot be wrong.
Below and facing page: *Simplicity of pose and a minimal use of props is the key to the appeal of these pictures.*
Above: *The gentle curve of the arch provides an effective frame for the picture.*

TRAVEL & HOLIDAY

TRAVEL AND HOLIDAY

When we travel to foreign climes, it is only natural that we wish to record the people as well as the landscape. Here again we are on difficult ground. Apart from those countries where the population believes the camera steals part of the soul, try to put yourself in the position of your intended subject. Imagine that a coachload of Ichibichi tribesmen arrives alongside your garden. All are intent upon capturing images of, say, Americans at their quaint old barbecue tradition. If your mental picture gets you going indoors for a shotgun, then don't be surprised if they reach for a spear. Likewise, a primitive indian dressed in a check golf jacket – and not much else – may look hysterically funny and worthy of 1/60 sec at f2.8. Yet to this man, amongst his own people, the old jacket is a status symbol. Laughingly to photograph him is to remove his dignity.

Assuming you have a guide who speaks the lingo, get the man's permission and let him pose in his own way. Don't offer money unless the guide thinks this is necessary. To say thank you and smile is much better P.R. for the next photographer who happens along. If any of your group carries a Polaroid camera, a print handed over is a nice gesture of thanks. Few of us are proficient in more than one extra language, yet, in spite of this, it

Canon F-1 35mm SLR camera with TTL metering. Optional automatic exposure facility, fitted with 200mm f2.8 telephoto lens.

Shooting into the light in *seascapes and other water scenes is common practice. Straightforward metering produces silhouetted forms, and reflections result in strong highlights. Sunset is the preferred time for such photographs, with the prevailing colour being dependent on the sky, and the weather conditions in general.*

TRAVEL & HOLIDAY

is often sufficient to know "please" and "thank you" in your host country's tongue in order to get along photographically. Proficiency in the old party game of dumb crambo can work wonders. To point at your camera then at your prospective subject, and ask "O.K.?," is invariably understood the world over, – as a hand waving to and fro across the body, accompanied by a verbal "Nao, non, nein, nyet" etc. should be self-evident to you. For those countries where the locals do not like being photographed, there are still tourist shows where national costumes are worn and photographs are expected to be taken.

Photojournalists resort to 90° lens attachments, shooting from the hip with a wide angle lens, or having a camera round the neck and a bulb release in the pocket – amongst other tricks. If, however, they get caught in the act, then getting arrested or having bricks thrown at them is part of the job. Most are competent sprinters!

I thoroughly recommend Magnum photographer Eve Arnold's book "In China," as a testament of how to photograph rich, humble, young and old, yet all with dignity and understanding.

Successful results in travel and holiday photography are related far more to application and foresight than to the quantity of photographic gear carried. Perhaps this is just as well. Whilst a touring trip in a camper may allow for several cases of equipment, the same journey in a Japanese "Compact" invariably means that the family's needs take precedence. The same applies to air travel, particularly those charter flights which will not allow excess baggage. Most of my lessons were learned during the five year period when I ran my own travel photographic library. I pass some of them on, in the hope that you do not have the same bad experiences, just fun – which is mostly what it is all about.

After my first commission, when I carried two 'underseat' outfit cases and a shoulder bag full of film – as cabin baggage – I learned to travel light. Needless to say this was in the late nineteen-sixties, before hi-jacking became the 'in' thing for various politically motivated nuts. Apart from current airline regulations over cabin baggage, there are also the problems of customs and X-ray machines. To deal with the former, it is better to look like a very amateur photographer. Bear in mind that many camera enthusiasts from affluent Western Nations own more photographic equipment than the top pro's of the poor country they are visiting. To take your entire armoury with you is asking for trouble: it will be assumed that you are a professional and therefore able to contribute to the host nation's upkeep.

Customs regulations in many countries were drafted pre-war, and can <u>still</u> be rigidly applied. Typically, the quantity of photographic gear allowed for "temporary importation" can be as follows:–

    1 x still camera and accessories
    1 x cine camera
    2 x rolls of film for each

(I am told that some countries will still specify:– Not more than twelve plates.)

Of course, a companion can double this technical allowance for you, but even so twenty-four plates do not go very far. Paying duty on extra gear and film is no fun. The reason for this is that cameras and film can easily cost several times as much as at home. To overcome any customs thoughts of resale, I remove 35mm film from its box and tape the label round the canister. Rollfilm too, can be removed from its box, if a maker's identification appears on the foil wrapping. Otherwise tear the entire top off the box. This seems to take care of being over quota. If you have to travel with a lot of equipment make a list (with serial numbers) and take several copies with you.

Forest and woodland scenes, *even on brilliantly sunny days, can be deceptively dark. So much so, that hand-held shots with the lens stopped down for depth, may be difficult. Use the trees themselves to steady the camera at slow shutter speeds. Make the most of the setting by observing the effects created by the light on your surroundings.* *Facing page: Views of the horizon in coastal shots can be made more interesting through the inclusion of foreground objects; these can be chosen simply for their shape. Maximum depth-of-field will aid the effect, and the use of hyperfocal distance and wide-angle lenses should be considered.*

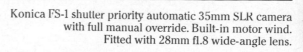

Konica FS-1 shutter priority automatic 35mm SLR camera with full manual override. Built-in motor wind. Fitted with 28mm f1.8 wide-angle lens.

Left: Firework displays can be photographed in basically two different ways. An instantaneous exposure can be used to show a single rocket burst, and whilst this will require a certain degree of anticipation, it is not difficult. Alternatively, with camera on tripod and shutter set open on 'B' several explosions can be captured.
Below: The Shrine of the Book, Jerusalem, photographed on Agfachrome 50S.

Photocopies of an insurance policy schedule are acceptable. This also helps to get your cameras through customs when you return home; particularly if your visit was to a camera buyers paradise. I keep my list of equipment (or carnet) handy when passing through customs, but do not offer it unless asked. For some reason, seaports seem to be more officious than airports. I once had to photograph a client's cruise ship, when it docked at the Mediterranean country where I was on location. Going through customs with necessarily a lot of gear, I was asked for a carnet – which was stamped, and a very cheerful customs official escorted me to where the ship was berthed. On the way back, there was only one bad tempered looking individual at the customs benches. He looked the sort of little guy whose domineering wife continuously said "no" during siesta. He was looking for trouble. Every item, down to the last lens hood, was taken out of my cases and checked against the carnet. The problem came when we got to my filters. On the carnet they were listed in quantity only. "Leest she no say Hoyas, you buy on sheep, you pay." I tried to explain that Hoyas were filters and not sold on ships. He was unconvinced and offered to confiscate if I didn't pay duty. At this point the penny dropped, so I asked "How much?" An hour's pantomime cost me a few drachmas. I didn't wait to see whether they went into the till or went to drown his sorrows.

I should perhaps explain, that one technically leaves the country when passing through the customs office. In theory you should carry a passport – even if going nowhere. I found this technicality rigidly enforced in both England and France when working on a car ferry account. The client required photographs of his ships entering and leaving harbour. On one occasion, the French stamped my passport six times in a day. To avoid any nonsense with customs, my client and I carried a camera each.

Half the film was in his briefcase, the rest in my pockets.

As with insurance, my philosophy with customs is to expect trouble. If you do it keeps away. Last year we went to Portugal for a holiday. I took a Hasselblad, three lenses, two magazines, a meter and fifteen rolls of film. I treated myself to a tan pigskin Hasselblad outfit case to hold the lot. Coming back through customs, we were stopped. You've guessed it – I had forgotten to carry bills, carnet or copy of my insurance policy. Next time I will take my own advice!

In the early days of in-flight terrorism, airport X–ray machines were installed as a panic measure, metal detectors following later. It is still stupid to put film into your main luggage, particularly if going to Israel or some Arab States. I have been told that X-ray film bags are an open invitation to turn up the wick to see what's inside. Many professional photographers now carry exposed film in a clear plastic bag through security control. The right to inspection, rather than seeing your camera case go through a machine, varies wildly from airport to airport. In some small countries, inspection is simply too much bother for officials – apart from the fact that you probably don't speak their language anyway. The clear plastic bag and a smile, seems to work better than insisting upon your "rights" with a bloody-minded official, toting a holstered .45, who couldn't care less if photography was the raison d'etre for your trip. There are no hard and fast rules about what happens to film if it is X-rayed. It depends upon the level at which the machine is set, as well as the cumulative effect of several doses, if passing through several countries. Black and white film will have a higher fog level which can sometimes be printed through. Colour negative film is the same, but with a colour cast that it may be possible to correct. The only X-rayed colour transparencies I have seen still had

Canon ML Autofocus. Automatic, programmed exposure 35mm viewfinder camera with 40mm f1.9 fixed lens.

The reading from a light meter provides a basis for exposure determination, and should not be blindly obeyed. The reflected-light meter will measure the average brightness of a scene, which, in night-time views that are composed of shadow and highlight, will mean a middle value that sacrifices both. The photographer must decide on the effect he wants, bearing in mind that whatever he does is essentially a compromise. The pictures shown on these pages demonstrate the photographers' interpretations of various night scenes, and the effect obtained when 'overexposing' for shadow detail, **left and bottom left,** 'underexposing' for the highlights, **bottom,** or using the 'correct' meter reading, **below.**

enough density left to enable me to make a black and white negative and print, thus providing a colleague with some record of his holiday. His camera of course was packed in his luggage, to free his hands for the more important purpose of carrying his duty free allowance and presents. Providing that you take elementary precautions over X-rays, the incidence of ruined film must now be very low. Tourism has become an important source of income to most countries in the world. Even emergent nations are beginning to realise that money has to come from somewhere.

Large 'glossy' outfit cases have always been an open invitation to the local thieves. Many professional travel

TRAVEL & HOLIDAY

Because there is plenty of light available, it does not mean that you cannot simulate night-time conditions. **Below:** *A short exposure and blue filter were used to create this pseudo-night shot, showing the desert rock forms in silhouette. The addition of a diffraction filter added a burst of colour and energy to an otherwise static scene.* **Bottom:** *A blue filter and carefully thought out composition were responsible*

for the feeling of isolation in this unusual 'night' shot. **Right:** *All is not what it seems, especially in photography, where imaginative double-exposure can create a haunting reality that does not in fact exist. To obtain this effect, the photographer shot the misty forest scene on film which he subsequently exposed to a torch shining through black card.* **Facing page:** *Lightning shots do not require matching reflexes. With camera mounted on tripod and pointing towards the action, set shutter to 'B' and keep it open until several flashes have elapsed. Aperture is not critical, but take several shots at different settings for best results.*

Polaroid SX-70 instant print reflex camera with Sonar AutoFocus system capable of focusing in total darkness.

photographers have given up the Learjet-Ferrari-Halliburton image in favour of padded canvas/nylon camera bags. This is more a question of keeping a low profile rather than being trendy, though dirty jeans, T-shirts, denim jackets and training shoes complete the image!

Whilst this generation of outfit bags does not give much protection against knocks, and is becoming more expensive than 'better' cases, they do have the huge advantage of being light. Carrying an eight pound alloy case around in 110°F temperature is no fun – even for a photographer's assistant – and by the time it is filled up with gear it can easily weigh twenty pounds or more. As a compromise, the Bach'O outfit cases are elegant, carry a lot of equipment and are expensive. I have two, but don't use them in hot climates, where a light coloured finish is essential in order to avoid heat absorption. A friend of mine covers his Bach'O cases with white plastic carrier bags for just this reason. They are easily slipped off when he wishes to open a case. A white garment thrown over a black case performs the same function. Pack a light coloured canvas camera or airline bag in your main luggage. Either will pack flat and take up little room. You can then divide your outfit as to needs when you arrive on location. My tripod

(less P & T head – which saves space) also goes in the main luggage, wrapped in plastic bubble sheeting, which protects both clothes and tripod. At one time, I also packed a 'cheapo' 300 or 500mm amongst the socks, shirts and pants, until an acquaintance of mine saw his 'bomb shaped' 300mm (in case) put into a bucket of water at a Spanish airport – he now carries a quality 2 x teleconverter instead!

Which film do you take on holiday? As mentioned earlier 'professional' films are out. Some films are more heat resistant than others, but this does not mean that they like being cooked in a car boot, or glove locker, or in a black case on the beach. I can only answer for both Kodachromes, amateur Ektachromes, Kodacolor II and 400, Agfachrome/color and Fujicolor as being good vacation films. Most normal black and white emulsions are quite safe. It is better to purchase fresh stock before departure. I do not advise purchase by post, as this can pre-cook films before you start. When the Kodak E6 films were announced, I rang Kodak's technical department for advice on which film to take on a projected trip to the Seychelles. They suggested ER120 as a direct replacement for the EX120 I had used for years. It was also suggested that I use a CC05 Green or CC10 Green filter to

TRAVEL & HOLIDAY

Subdued evening light can create a bewildering range of colours and moods. This may range from the rich red of a setting sun in a clear sky to the almost monochromatic greys of a rain-charged cloudscape. Creativity, however, does not end with observation. The overall feel of the picture can be influenced by careful exposure, and here the photographer's imagination must take over. Should you expose for high-lights, dark areas or simply for the whole scene? The choice is yours.

cancel any magenta bias caused by tropical heat. This advice was qualified, in that I should shoot a test film with and without filters before departure and get it processed at my usual lab. They were absolutely right. My lab was consistently running about .025 magenta, so a CC10 Green gave me the balance I liked. Most people prefer a warmer bias, so it may be that Kodachrome 64, Ektachrome ER and Fujicolor are just as you like them – without filtration. I should add that the CC10G filter replaced my usual Hoya IB filter. I have tried Ektachrome professional (EPR) in hot conditions as an experiment. The colour cast varied between batches and was much stronger than on Ektachrome ER. Colour negative films are no problem, though I would not use Vericolor II in preference to Kodacolor for a long trip.

What camera/s you use is really a matter of personal taste, but remember that a Mamiya RB67 with pentaprism gets really heavy after a while. I sold my Pentax 6 x 7 for the same reason. Since I like large transparencies, I now have a Plaubel 67 which weighs in about the same as my Leica R3 and seems to take up less space when folded. Its wide angle lens (about the same angle of view as 35mm on 35mm) is ideal for stock shots. I prefer chrome to black finished 35mm SLR's since they heat up less, though to be fair, my black Pentax did a lot of travelling without giving unexpected results due to heat.

My old M2 Leicas have been used in very hot and very cold conditions, still keep on working and don't need batteries. With a collapsible wide angle lens, they will easily fit under an old ski

jacket – or in an anorak pocket. One is equipped with a rare (but fortunately not valuable) Benser baseplate, which carries any two of 35mm, 50mm or 90mm lenses. The latter makes a good carrying handle! Whilst this baseplate needs to be unscrewed with a small coin in order to change film, since I usually also carry a second body this has not proved to be a problem. A similar device could be made up for many modern 35mm SLR's.

Ski buffs tell me that it is not a good idea to ski with a camera under a jacket, as this is a quick way to get bad chest injuries should you fall. There are now derriere camera pouches available which are much safer for use by motor-cyclists and climbers as well. The alternative route is to carry a Rollei 35, Minox/Ricoh folder or Olympus XA in a side pocket. In the past I have used a Retina IIIC and a post-war 16 on 120 Zeiss Ikonta. The latter is barely larger than the former but gives bigger transparencies. The modern Chinese "Seagull" 6 x 6cm folder, would be a cheap alternative for bigger format enthusiasts.

One of my favourite winter sports accessories is a small sledge. These can be hired at most resorts, and are ideal for carting a camera case and tripod around in the snow. A couple of elastic motorcycle luggage straps keep things secure. I first discovered this when a client wanted dusk or dawn shots of resorts in the Austrian Tyrol. Having once done large format photography in the snow, I also remembered to take three 6″ square pieces of alloy sheet to spread the load of the tripod legs, which will otherwise sink during a time exposure. It is quite

exciting to sit on the sledge and 'motor' back to the resort afterwards.

If the weather is cold, watch out for condensation on lenses and viewfinders. If it is really cold, watch out for batteries ceasing to work.

My last thought about travel photography concerns the attitude of officialdom in some countries towards 'espionage' or national security. For instance, it is not a good idea to photograph uniformed individuals without permission, unless they happen to be wearing ceremonial attire. Politically sensitive nations, and all Eastern Bloc States, are a bit paranoiac about people taking pictures of power stations or waterworks, or even state banks. Certainly anything surrounded with barbed wire and notices should not be included in your photographic itinerary. A former assistant of mine, on assignment for the Government of a Middle Eastern State, was arrested by the military for photographing a gibbet against a sunset. Despite the fact that he was working for the Ministry of Tourism, his film was still confiscated, without reason being given.

In spite of mentioning some negative aspects of travel photography in this chapter – and I didn't even get around to flies, inoculations or snakes! – I do know that most of us photographers find that our old pictures become more precious as the years pass. To have lost the record of even part of a trip through lack of knowledge, or by not having taken a few precautions, could well remain a matter of regret.

NATURE & CLOSE UPS

NATURE AND CLOSE-UPS

Nature photography, often of necessity, becomes an available light subject, since so many creatures and plants need a sheltered and therefore photographically dark habitat. The temptation to use flash is always present. Yet to do so, in the interests of clarity – or desperation – easily destroys the natural ambience. The end result is a photograph for science not of art. Of course, either approach to the subject is perfectly valid, and frequently the use of flash is the only alternative to no picture at all. Nocturnal creatures fit into this category. Most animals and birds, when startled by flash, suffer an involuntary bowel movement. This can be very unfortunate for the photographer setting off a caveful of bats, where an umbrella is a useful accessory! Many insect photographers go to great lengths in building indoor sets in order to produce a photograph with some resemblance to natural lighting and subject environment. The use of high speed electronic flash units, triggered when the insect crosses a light beam, have produced some remarkably 'natural' pictures of insects in flight. This equipment is now available at an affordable price. I once tried to photograph the humming-bird hawk moth (Macroglossum Stellatarum) in its natural habitat. The 1/2000 sec shutter speed of my Nikon F2 was nowhere near fast enough to stop the moth's wing movement to an acceptable degree.

By contrast, taking nature pictures by available light will of necessity mean fast film and wide lens apertures, yet this in itself can produce beautiful pictures. To concentrate the plane of sharpness upon an insect's head, flower stamen, or a cat's eyes or whiskers, can produce a softer effect without any distracting background detail. Furry animals, in particular, look even fluffier when limited depth of field is used. Butterflies can be photographed from above – or from the side, with folded wings – at surprisingly large apertures, yet will still retain enough depth of field and definition. Within this 'romantic' genre of nature pictures, a certain amount of grain does not become objectionable, indeed colour grain adds to the feeling. I regularly push ASA 400 reversal material by ⅔rds to 1 stop extra. Part of this is to allow for the fact that subjects photographed under trees, or other foliage, take on a green cast. Pushing reversal colour films tends to alter the colour balance towards yellow. So we then arrive at a situation of having to filter out a yellow-green cast. For this reason, I normally push ASA ratings to allow for the correction filter factor, as much as for reasons of an adequate shutter speed. To a certain extent, any filter correction depends upon the film to be used. A magenta biased emulsion, such as Fujichrome, helps a lot under these conditions. Otherwise a CC20 magenta or red gelatin filter provides at least a starting point. Many photographers use a brown 81 series filter with Ektachrome or Kodachrome when working under trees. This is a cliché, derived from glamour photography, when an 81 filter does help with caucasian skin tones. For other subjects, red or magenta filters give a more accurate colour rendering.

Photography of birds is highly specialised. The experts have spent a lifetime studying both the subject and the photographic means of recording it. One photographer, Eric Hosking, even lost an eye by getting too keen over one of his subjects. This did not deter him. As far back as the 1890's, photographer Cherry Kearton and his naturalist brother Richard, climbed trees and cliffs – complete with a half plate camera and tripod. In one of their books, there are illustrations showing how to descend a cliff with the aforesaid camera suspended over one shoulder. Pictures of elaborate 'hides' abound, as well as one entitled "Great Skua attacking watcher." Another is captioned "Fishing boats

The colours of nature change with the seasons, weather and the time of day. **Below and facing page:** *The cold, misty light of a winter morning has much to offer the photographer keen enough to venture forth. An eerie calm covers the sleeping countryside, the cool, diffused rays of a low sun softening and reducing to tones of grey, green and brown all that they touch. Taking close-up shots of nature can become a hobby in itself, indeed, many*

photographers concentrate their efforts on flowers, plants or insects to the exclusion of all other subjects. Bellows units, extension rings, macro and close-up lenses are all useful devices at the enthusiasts disposal, although the latter are amongst the cheapest, and require no exposure adjustment in the absence of TTL metering. A piece of white card to act as a reflector is a useful accessory that will help fill-in awkward shadows.

Soligor 35-70mm f2.5 macro-focus zoom lens, available in a variety of fittings.

The outdoor scene in winter frequently appears bereft of colour. Snow-covered landscapes with their bare trees, **facing page,** can be shown for what they are, with under- exposure heightening the sombre mood. On clear days, the sun itself can become a point of focus, tinting the surroundings with its rich glow.

photographed at midnight in the Shetlands." The quality of these pictures would be hard to match today.

Having given a very brief indication of what's involved in going at the subject whole hog, is it necessary to go this far to photograph the odd bird or squirrel in the back garden? One of the nicest presents my wife and I have been given was a bird table. Positioned about fifteen feet from our kitchen window, it has given us many hours of pleasure watching the odd bird or squirrel frequenting a fixed spot. By putting out food regularly, we have encouraged the local wild life to visit our garden. After three years, we now receive visits from unusual, if not rare, birds. From our kitchen window it is possible, with a cheap 500mm lens, to record our 'visitors' in close-up without suffering the discomfort of a hide. We also have nesting boxes, coconuts, peanuts and meat fat or bones within camera range of the house. Since it is no effort to use a heavy tripod, exposures down to ⅛ or even ¼ sec are possible during the winter.

Photography in zoos by available light does mean a fast film and lens. With 35mm format, my favourite is a 180mm or 200mm f2.8 lens. For 6 x 6cm a 250mm or 300mm f4 is the fastest around, but it is possible to use ASA 400 film and still get a good quality blow-up. Using a fast lens wide open does mean that the

limited depth of field can 'lose' bars, netting and distracting backgrounds. Don't worry about shooting into the light, as this makes furry creatures look more so, but don't forget to compensate your exposure. Dark animals, like some bears, absorb a lot of light. It is as well to carry artificial light balanced film, if you intend to work indoors. Zoos invariably use tungsten lighting, rather than fluorescent, since this helps to keep up the temperature. A macro lens and 160 ASA colour film will enable fish enthusiasts to hand hold in an aquarium. I prefer to use a 100mm macro with a rubber lens hood. This can be put up against the glass tank, thus avoiding reflections. Some tissues are useful for cleaning off other people's fingerprints from the tank before shooting. Lens cleaning fluid is more efficient than saliva in a bad case, and is no effort to carry in a gadget bag or pocket.

Open air zoos (in particular) and safari parks, guarantee that many interesting animals will be far away. I find that in these places I take more shots on 400mm or 500mm lenses than on 200mm or 300mm focal lengths. For 'bigheads' I find a tele-converter useful, stretching my 500mm to 1000mm. My wife's shoulder is often used as a lens brace to avoid camera shake. When she is not with me I have to carry a tripod!

Since so much nature photography is either close-up or at a distance, a reflex camera is preferable, though there is one exception. Before embarking on macro or tele-photography, check that your favourite SLR does not give image cut-off with bellows or long lenses. Whilst this will not appear on the film, it can make subject framing very difficult. For similar reasons a camera with interchangeable focusing screens is preferable. Central rangefinder and microprism focusing aids can become unusable, giving an annoying dead area in the centre of the screen. Check the camera maker's list of interchangeable screens, to see which suits you and your projected equipment best. The exception to the SLR, mentioned earlier, is the Leitz Visoflex mirror box attachment for rangefinder Leicas. First made over forty years ago, the Viso has a very long mirror to avoid cut-off, and gives an extremely bright image – particularly with the

NATURE & CLOSE UPS

straight magnifier. Unlike the optional 90° pentaprism viewfinder though, you are coping with a laterally reversed image, but this is not important in practice. Another advantage of the Visoflex with straight magnifier, is that it is possible to focus at f22 under reasonable lighting conditions. I know of no SLR which can do this without a special aerial image focusing screen, and many photographers are unable to use these with comfort. The Visoflex is not expensive when purchased secondhand, though you will need a Leica body to go with it!

Whether to use extension rings or bellows is largely a matter of intended use. Cheap extension rings will not give automatic diaphragm operation, and very few will give TTL exposure metering except in the stopped-down mode. On balance, the bellows unit is more versatile and frequently cheaper. It is certainly easier to use when reproduction ratios are variable. Against this, only the expensive models retain automatic diaphragm operation, though an accessory control ring and double cable release can restore this feature at a reasonable cost. When focusing a close-up, it is easier to move the whole camera unit. When working from a tripod, accessory racking units are available, which fit between tripod and camera to perform just this function.

Hexanon 85mm f1.8 long-focus lens for Konica cameras.

The choice of lenses for use in close-up work is pretty wide. Beginning with a standard 50mm lens of from f1.2 to f2 aperture is where most of us start. A wide aperture standard lens is not designed to work at close distances. Very few will perform well when used with either extension rings or close-up lenses. Generally, the wider the maximum aperture, the poorer the close-up performance will be. Many f1.2 and f1.4 lenses can barely be focused when fitted with a strong close-up lens of three or four dioptres. Most camera makers produce a reversing ring to enable a lens to be fitted back to front on the camera. This usually gives a subject ratio of around natural size, and will provide adequate definition. A cable release operated diaphragm control ring can also be purchased for convenience. Metering will be through the stop down method.

It is far better to use a 50 or 55mm macro lens for reproduction ratios down to half or natural size. Many photographers use a macro as a standard lens, particularly the generation of internal focusing lenses, which retain high corrections at infinity as well as close-ups. The 'longer' macros of 100mm and 200mm focal length allow more room between subject and camera. This allows space for lighting the subject as well as reducing the tendency to photograph in your own shadow. These lenses are lovely to use but tend to be big and expensive. All macro lenses stop down farther than normal lenses, which gives increased depth of field.

Top left: A crisp frost on a cold winter's morning coats the trees with a delicate white foliage, with strong backlighting enhancing the effect. Left: Mist diffuses the sunlight and creates a soft background for the trees. Bottom: A wide-angle lens was used to emphasise the feeling of solitude and draw attention to the clouds. Facing page top: An object as simple as a gate was given impact by the white surroundings. Bottom: The melting ice of a frozen lake reflects irregular patterns of shimmering light.

There is also a generation of macro lenses with very short focal lengths. These are intended for use with bellows units and give larger than life-sized images. If you wish to photograph a bee's knees, these are for you. They are made by most of the famous lens makers and are expensive. Budget 35mm focal length macros are made by Spiratone and Novoflex. None of these ultra macros have automatic diaphragms, or facility to fit same.

Leica thread enlarger lenses are very good for close-ups, and can be easily fitted to most cheap bellows units. My favourite is the 105mm Nikkor, which when fitted to a bellows unit will focus from infinity to same size. It will also stop down to f45! For closer than about 1:1, enlarger lenses should also be used reversed for critical work. Enlarger lenses with Leica 39mm thread are obtainable in focal lengths of from one to six inches. The only lenses which I have found unsuitable for macro work, are those flat field enlarger lenses which are designed to be used at or near maximum aperture.

Long focus 90 and 135mm Leitz lenses could be unscrewed from their focusing mounts, and used in a bellows unit with a special screw thread adaptor. Similar lens heads are available

NATURE & CLOSE UPS

Bottom right: A large expanse of sky, with exposure made for the brightest area, created this simple, yet powerful outline against a spectrum-coloured backdrop. Right: Under-exposure of the subject resulted in a silhouette of the fisherman that conveys particularly well the impression of effort. Far right: This scene was exposed to show detail in the group of buildings, allowing foreground to fade into shadow. Below: A daylight shot, grossly under-exposed, created a night-time look. Facing page: A red sky, the mist-enshrouded bridge and home-bound cars on a winter's evening; each picture creates a different feeling.

from Leitz to this day. I have an old 9cm coated Elmar lens which makes a superb bellows lens. It was not expensive and can also be used on my screw Leica!

Several other lens makers also produce short mount bellows lenses of 90 or 100mm focal length. I have used both Nikon and Novoflex products with superb results. The lenses which do not work well for macro use are telephotos, wide angles and large format lenses (unless special apochromats). I am not too keen on macro-zooms either – except as a compromise – for two reasons. Firstly, I found the lens very clumsy for close distances when not using a tripod, and secondly, the definition was awful when used stopped right down in order to get enough depth of field. I must say in all fairness, that flower studies taken at three stops down were acceptable and not of as low contrast as expected.

Medium format users too, can enjoy the fascination of close-up photography, though bellows units are the rule and horribly expensive. I would dearly love a Hasselblad macro lens of say 80 to 100mm focal length and f4 aperture – I have even asked them to produce one, without success. The Mamiya RB67 does now have a macro lens available, which should be quite something. As a cost compromise, I own an old Practisix and bellows unit, which together with my 80mm Nikkor enlarging lens produces nice close-up transparencies. The lack of TTL metering is not really a problem as long as one remembers to allow for inverse square law. This sounds horrifying but in practice is simple. It translates into photographic terms as follows:–

We begin by understanding that a lens, when extended from

Kodak Ektachrome 400. 400 ASA daylight-balanced colour transparency film. Available in 35mm and 120 rolls.

its marked focal length to a distance of twice its focal length – or double extension in large format terms – requires not twice the exposure in compensation but <u>four</u> times. It is easy to draw a graph with exposure factor to 4x on one axis, and camera extension to 2x on the other axis. Half stop increases in exposure can then be related to bellows (or extension tube) length. You can, of course, extrapolate the graph as far as you like, once you have drawn it out. For practical purposes, lens extension is measured from the film plane marking on the camera, to the iris diaphragm of the lens. I carry a small piece of card in my camera case with the details written out, together with a small length of dressmaker's tape measure.

The Practisix table reads:–

Extension	Exposure Increase
80mm	0
100mm	½ stop
120mm	1 stop
140mm	1½ stops
160mm	2 stops
200mm	2½ stops

I have tables for my large format lenses too. There are people who produce these figures on a pocket calculator, and though same is not part of my normal photographic equipment, it may well suit you to do it this way.

Large format users are more into flora than fauna though, as mentioned, this was not always the case. The amount of detail allied with real tonal quality has proved to be the attraction of the big negative or transparency. Grossbild photographers are very disciplined – they have to be. Bracketing means that three times the number of darkslides have to be carried. To guard against accidents, it is usual to shoot two 'normal' exposures, processing one sheet and 'holding' one sheet in case compensation in processing is necessary. Whilst, to a certain extent, a polaroid test can ascertain exposure, this technique tends to be the province of studio, rather than location, photographers, the latter being conscious of extra weight in a back pack. Lightweight large format cameras such as the Nagaoka and Ikeda have been largely responsible for this new trend, inspired no doubt by the work of Weston and Adams, who really did it the hard way. For photography of trees and plants, virtually any modern multi-coated lens is suitable. The new infinity computed apochromats from Nikon and Fujica have an appreciable edge over older designs. For reasonable lighting conditions, their modest f9 maximum aperture is of no disadvantage.

For real close-up work, the symmetrical (or near symmetrical) Symmar, Nikkor, or Sironar, Dagor or Fujinon are more than adequate performers, though for ultimate results, I would go for an apochromatic process lens which is specially designed to work at close distances. It is also possible to use a reversed enlarger lens, mounted in a shutter, for extreme macro work. Large format users live with the inverse square law through necessity; and find it no problem. Some 5 x 4″ format cameras have the facility for fitting a 120 rollfilm adaptor back. Arca and Sinar cameras can use a maker's back which will hold a Hasselblad, Bronica or various 35mm SLR bodies to provide a massive bellows extension. Arca still make a 5 x 4″ reflex camera which will couple to their monorail. Cambo and Gowland produce 5 x 4″ format twin lens reflex cameras. None of these attachments or cameras are really suited to location photography, yet, no doubt, someone will disagree and have beautiful results to prove it!

PROCESSING

PROCESSING BLACK AND WHITE

We all talk glibly about 'pushing' an ASA 400 film to ASA 800, 1600, 3200 and so on, simply because this is the way our camera or exposure meter is scaled. In fact, when pushing any film – whether black and white or colour – it is correct to quote not ASA but an E.I. (or Exposure Index) figure. The reason for this is that an ASA rating is calculated from the ability of a negative (or transparency) to 'hold' a number of tones. The original subject is a stepped scale with tones ranging from white, through greys, to black. Optimum exposure and development will reproduce a range of tones to a 128:1 ratio – or seven stops. When an emulsion can reproduce this scale of tones, then it is possible to arrive at a speed rating – expressed as an ASA figure. This is further complicated by a factor known as gamma – or the contrast ratio between white and black.

What happens when we start to increase development time, in order to push a film beyond its rated speed, is that contrast increases. The original grey scale becomes progressively compressed, until we are left with virtually only black and white plus a high fog level – which is an inevitable side effect of over-extended development. By the time this state of affairs is reached, we are no longer talking about an ASA rating, since the range of tones has been so drastically reduced. In practice, E.I. ratings end

when a negative becomes unprintable, and a transparency becomes a monochromatic sick green joke.

How far can one push a black and white negative? Here we have three variables, namely: subject contrast, emulsion contrast and developer contrast – just to make life complicated. Subject contrast, as mentioned in a previous chapter, can have a ratio way above the recording capabilities of any emulsion. To save you flipping back through the pages, let me remind you that subject contrast varies from a ratio of 2,000,000:1, for a landscape with sun 'in shot', to 2:1 for the same landscape without sun, and misty – to cloud the issue! Fortunately, most daylight subjects will fit within the optimum seven stop ratio.

When we come to emulsion contrast, you can take it as read that the faster films are of lower contrast, and the slower films of higher contrast, with FP4 and Plus X somewhere near the middle.

When it comes to developers, at the high contrast end we have all those print developers, which can be used for films, and Kodak's DK50 and D19 (really an X-ray developer), which are primarily for sheet film and 2475/Royal X Pan emulsions. Developers like the traditional ID11 and D76 fine grain formulae (virtually identical) form the medium contrast category, together with the high acutance developers like Paterson's Acutol. Low contrast developers are, perhaps surprisingly, of two opposing types. On the one hand, there are speed reducing ultra fine grain

Ilford HP5. 400 ASA black and white negative film.
Available in 35mm and 120 rolls.

developers like Kodak Microdol X and Ilford Perceptol, and on the other, speed increasing developers such as Ilford Microphen, Paterson Acuspeed, Edwal FG7 and many others.

Having briefly examined the parameters, we now return to the original question of "How far can one push a black and white film?" Subject contrast is largely decided by what we find and what we wish to record. Most available light subjects are of high contrast. Because we wish to work in this genre of pictures, the camera is inevitably loaded with fast film. At this point – not later – we have to decide upon the exposure and development which will give the desired result. Hypothetically, the choice is that we can give a normally rated exposure and use a speed increasing developer to increase shadow detail, or we can 'uprate' the ASA setting – because the lighter toned subject areas are more important, or because our metered shuttered speed is insufficient to stop subject movement. Either way, we are limited to around a one stop push, if any degree of tonality is to be retained. If grain is not a major factor, and we have a good supply of grade 'O' bromide paper, then up to four stops push is possible. It is no accident that speed increasing developers are of low contrast. By extending development time, we increase contrast, so by starting at a low contrast chemical situation, we have something in hand – like one stop in ASA terms. After this, we are into E.I. ratings.

Facing page, left and bottom: Despite the corrected colour rendering that tungsten film gives under most types of artificial light, many photographers opt for the warmer effect that is the characteristic of daylight emulsions. An 80B blue filter can be used to correct the response of daylight film, but this has the disadvantage of losing a valuable stop. **Top left:** An imposing backdrop prompted the photographer to retain the silhouette-like subject rendering in this shot, as compensation for backlighting would have destroyed the architectural detail.

As mentioned earlier, the chromogenic Agfa Vario-XL and Ilford XPI would seem to be the answer to an available light photographer's prayer. To a certain extent they are, and this is one of the reasons why they are now on the market. Perhaps a short word of explanation will make the situation clearer. All colour films contain three black and white layers, chromogenic films have two, and 'normal' films one layer. Forgetting for the moment the trade processing advantages of chromogenics, the fact that they contain two emulsions allows a high degree of contrast control, greater exposure latitude and an increase in maximum emulsion speed. You may remember the relative speed of 1935 Kodachrome compared to contemporary black and white films, mentioned in a previous chapter. This is how chromogenics can attain a true ASA 1600 rating and retain fine grain and gradation. Like for everything else in life, there is always a price to pay. Chromogenics end up more expensive by the time you hold the negatives in your hand, whether you use a trade house or do it yourself. The base coloration of Ilford XPI will mean longer exposure times in the enlarger, though rumour

PROCESSING

has it that Ilford are changing this. Big enlargement enthusiasts would do better to process their own films, since the cleanliness of trade C41 processing leaves a lot to be desired. 120 enthusiasts will have fewer spotting problems than their 35mm confrères! High processing temperatures can be difficult to maintain where winter is cold.

Before moving on to push processing colour films, just a short word about the techniques of latensification and hyper-sensitising. The former requires a carefully controlled pre-exposure of the film through neutral density filters in order to raise the level of threshold densities – or in common parlance, to

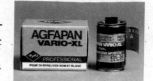

Available light is the preferred medium of many professional glamour and nude photographers. This may be the oblique sunlight streaming through an open window, diffused backlighting or the subdued light of a darkened room. Even those photographers who work exclusively in the controlled conditions of a studio often devise methods of simulating available light conditions. Tracing paper hung over an open doorway and illuminated by a photoflood in reflector from behind, is one such simple system. The final effect should be chosen to match the model.

COLOUR

How far can you push a colour negative film? The short answer is one stop. Beyond this, grain and colour rendering reach an unacceptable level. Of course, what is unacceptable is necessarily a subjective matter. Critique or criticism may well state respectively "The amorphous highlight quality subtends a feeling of intrinsic harmony, and sensuality towards the compositional planes," or simply "What went wrong?" To this end, it is possible to push ASA 400 colour film up to an E.I. of 10,000. Whether you like the result or not is a matter of honesty, not technique or critique. By comparison, most E6 colour reversal emulsions seem to thrive on modest degrees of push. I can assure you that many professional photographers habitually push half a stop in order to 'clean up' a white background. This is a matter of increasing contrast more than anything else; to counteract colour

ractionally increase shadow detail. Hypersensitising amounts to he same thing, only in this case mercury fumes are used to artially fog a film before exposure. Mercury fumes are very angerous to people and produce unpredictable results. In either ase, the effective ASA speed rating is unlikely to be increased by nore than 50%, and if used in conjunction with a 'speed brew,' vill only produce a higher fog level. Unless you have a scientific ent, stay with convention – it's safer!

PROCESSING

shift towards yellow, a blue filter would have been used at the time of exposure. On the other hand, these professionals are dealing with a static studio situation, where the subject remains stationary between tests. Since most reversal colour materials are now E6 compatible, it is probably safe to quote Kodak's modified processing data which allows a maximum two stop push, but nevertheless qualifies "If these losses in quality can be tolerated." Few labs care to push colour transparencies beyond two stops (yellow bias plus increased contrast) or cut more than half a stop (shift to blue plus lower contrast). If your local friendly lab still has an E6 hand line, they may be prepared (for a price) to go beyond these limits. Otherwise, it is all down to you. Most professional E6 labs will push or cut in third stop increments, if exposure is this critical. This, of course, assumes a test roll or clip test for evaluation, before final instruction is given. Unless you know your camera extremely well, it is not advisable to go straight into modified processing without this assurance.

Since the demise of GAF500, it has become difficult to produce the Seurat inspired pointillist effects of Sarah Moon and other photographers. Perhaps the new 3M 650T will restore this technique to our photographic armoury.

INTENSIFICATION AND REDUCTION

Once upon a time, when God was a boy and Johnsons of Hendon hadn't been taken over, there existed a range of photographic products called "Pactums." Even schoolboys like myself, could afford the sum these trial-sized packs cost. Each weekend, amateur photographers could purchase a different developer, toner, reducer or intensifier to play with. Even the professionals that I knew in those happy days kept a secret store of "amateur" Pactum intensifiers and reducers, just for those jobs where a few fluid ounces and fewer pence could save the shot.

Just as in those far off days, intensification should primarily be used for under developed negatives. Under exposure correction is limited to about half a stop, which really isn't worth the effort. All of us, sooner or later, however, suffer from the sort of mental abberation which produces a roll of thin flat negatives. It could be that HP5 was developed for the shorter Pan F time, or we misread the time and temperature chart, thermometer, or even the clock. Then there is mixing up development times between

Kodak Tri-X Pan. 400 ASA black and white negative film. Available in 35mm and 120 rolls.

diluted and undiluted solution; to say nothing of development in stale chemicals etc, etc.

Before starting any chemical after treatment, it is always advisable to try and print the most important negatives. If they are lacking in contrast, don't worry, because a print which is a grade soft is fine for copying. Any intensification (or reduction) process entails a degree of risk to the negative, and quite often a print from a copy negative can be better than that from an intensified original. Before doing anything else, make sure that the negatives to be intensified are thoroughly washed. Residual fixer – particularly rapid fixer – can ruin an otherwise salvable negative. It is also advisable to cut rollfilm into manageable lengths and use dishes for the solutions, because to try and intensify a whole roll in a tank is asking for trouble. The next stage is to take a negative from the same batch as those for intended intensification, and try the process.

Nowadays, it seems that only Chromium intensifier is commercially available. This does have the advantage of not being poisonous, and in a packet formula does not need an acid constituent. Like all intensification processes which are in the bleach, wash and re-develop category, there is a big increase in grain as well as contrast. The reason for this is that fine grain developers are not vigorous enough, so something akin to a print

developer must be used. Chromium intensifier can also be used on prints, and the process can be repeated a second time for a slight further increase in density. Agitation should be constant. Other intensifiers which can be mixed up only from raw chemicals are: Copper – freckle sized grain and odd brown colour image; Uranium – now virtually unobtainable for obvious reasons; and various lethal solutions containing mercuric iodide and potassium cyanide. These latter are unlikely to be supplied by the local chemist, even if he knows how fond you are of the mother-in-law!

Much the same technique applies to the use of a reducer. Ferricyanide (or Farmer's) reducer seems to be the only formula currently on sale. Since it contains hypo as the activator, a negative intended for treatment must first be thoroughly washed. A dry negative should be given a good pre-soak in water. Any Pot. Ferri. reducer will attack the negative shadow areas first. The stronger the solution colour, the quicker the action. It is much better to work with a weaker solution and take your time. As with intensification, practice on a spare negative and give constant agitation to the solution. Take the negative out of the reducer at frequent intervals, and wash briefly in water before examining for density reduction. Farmer's reducer can also be used on prints. Again, keep the solution weak and rinse frequently.

PRINTING

PRINTING

Mix-it-yourself enthusiasts can use what is called a proportional reducer, i.e. one which attacks the dense silver areas of a negative before having a go at the shadows. These formulae contain potassium permanganate and/or ammonium per-sulphate, or ferric sulphate, together with nothing more dangerous than weak sulphuric acid. Distilled or rain water must be used to make up all proportional reducers. Formulae and full working instructions can be found in most old photography books – which are still inexpensive if you look around.

In the late nineteen sixties, there was an up and coming photographer who, by repute, produced the sharpest black and white prints in London. Quite often people could not recall his work, but they always remembered his amazing print quality.

As I happened to know him rather well, I was frequently asked by other photographers for details of his secret process. Nobody believed me when I told them the truth. Here it is for you now. His negatives were produced by normal cameras, on normal films and developed in normal Kodak brew, just as the manu-facturers recommended. He printed on a somewhat crudely home-built enlarger, complete with a cardboard negative carrier, which would have been a joke to an amateur, let alone a professional. A cheap nineteen fifties Dallmeyer enlarger lens – which came unscrewed with great regularity, provided the optical excellence. His enlarger timer was an old clock, which clanked out the seconds when turned on its side, and to cap it all, his basement darkroom was not only damp but also haunted. Yes, honestly!

His "secret" certainly wasn't his equipment or even the influence of the malevolent spirit. He did not waste lots of paper to get <u>THE</u> print – he couldn't afford to. But what he did have, and still has, is infinite patience. As an equipment freak, I have often to remind myself that the newer, bigger, better and inevitably more expensive piece of darkroom gear, that I hanker after, still won't make me any better as a printer.

EQUIPMENT

Enlargers come in all shapes and sizes, from flimsy folding devices – for those who need to print the odd espionage neg – to giant structures which Brunel would have been proud of. Obviously the amount of space available is of paramount importance, but there are instances where a little ingenuity can solve this problem. I know a Leica main dealer who has a very cramped basement darkroom and a very big enlarger. In order to indulge in his passion for giant prints, he cut a hole in the darkroom ceiling which allowed his enlarger head to rise to a position under the counter in the shop above. A quick boxing-in job made the whole thing light tight and out of sight.

There is a lot to be said for buying an enlarger which will handle negatives bigger than 35mm. Sooner or later most photographers will want to print a 6 x 6cm or larger negative. For years I have used "universal" enlargers, which give me a choice of format from 6 x 9cm down to half frame. My original Gnome Alpha was fitted to the wall on a longer than standard column. A baseboard, which could be fixed at different levels, allowed for big degrees of enlargement. This was just as well, as I only owned 50mm and 105mm lenses – which had to cope with everything. I purchased a secondhand MPP Universal enlarger when I became interested in colour, and needed a filter drawer facility. I still have this enlarger in my home darkroom along with a vintage Leitz Valoy. In the studio, we have expensive modern enlargers, though I must say in all honesty, that for all their convenience, style and smoothness of the controls, they don't

Ilford XP1. 400 ASA nominal rating chromogenic black and white negative film. Wide latitude enables exposure at between 50-1600 E.I. Available in 35mm and 120 rolls.

produce any sharper prints. It is undoubtedly reactionary to say that I neither like nor trust automatic focus enlargers. Yes, they are very convenient and I wouldn't say "no" to a Leitz V 35 for a Christmas present, but as long as I am not happy using them, then this is reason enough for not having one at home.

There are several other considerations to be made when choosing an enlarger. Does one need a filter drawer if there is no intention of making colour prints? Well, this facility can also carry a piece of ground or flashed opal glass, which is a lovely way to reduce printing contrast – and increase print exposure time! We use this in the studio for printing contrasty EI 1250 symposium negatives, as well as a means of reducing contrast when making Cibachromes. Flashed opal may give a colour cast. An expedient alternative is to use a matt acetate, like a section of a 5 x 4" transparency sleeve. Most photographers will agree that glass negative carriers are an abomination. Apart from the danger of Newton's rings, there are also six surfaces to keep free of dust, and I for one, do not enjoy spotting prints anymore than the next photographer. Even anti-Newton glass won't help you here, and can impart an anti-Newton pattern on to a large, or section of negative, type print.

In the upper echelons of the enlarger world, there are still cold cathode light sources available. These are useless for colour, but worth considering for habitually contrasty black and white negatives. The contrast difference is about one grade of paper softer when compared with a conventional condenser enlarger head.

Reflex heads tend to have slightly lower contrast than 'normal' old-fashioned double condenser units, no doubt because it's all done with mirrors. Most colour heads tend to be softer still – some can even match cold cathode for lack of contrast. There are now so many dial-in colour heads on the market that I can only suggest you try before you buy – if possible.

As yet, I only know of one Multigrade head for professional enlargers. Should the system catch on this time around, it won't be long before smaller units are made.

When it comes to a choice of enlarger lens, go for the best you can afford. If necessary, buy an enlarger which is cheaper than the lens. A cheap enlarger can usually be squared up – a cheap lens cannot. One route to buying a quality lens at a reasonable cost, is to look around the secondhand field, but beware. For some unknown reason, enlarger lenses always seem to have had a hard life. Photographers who care greatly for their cameras and lenses, seem to have no compunction in cleaning an enlarger lens with a shirt sleeve or tail. Every so often one will come across an apparent bargain, only to find that the lens has been in the hypo or been splashed with something even nastier. Darkrooms can be mucky places, so enlarger lenses should live in the 'lamp' or in their little plastic boxes, not on a bench. A medium priced lens from a well known maker like Schneider, Rodenstock or Minolta, is a good compromise. Although you will have to stop down further in order to pull in the corners of a big enlargement, the longer exposure necessary here must be balanced against the alternative of a greater outlay for a "better" lens. Amongst the top quality enlarger lenses are the new generation of wide angles. With a focal length of around 20% less than normal, these optics allow for an enlarger with a shorter column and therefore more compact dimensions, whilst still permitting enlargements of a good size. Because of the high degree of optical correction necessary in any wide angle design, these lenses are necessarily expensive.

Contact printing is not yet a dead art, indeed there are signs of its resurgence in America. With the growth of interest in large format cameras, some of this is no doubt in emulation of the greats, whose art prints now fetch art prices. On a more mundane level, most of us who haven't learned to "read" negatives still make a contact print to see what masterpieces we haven't produced. Equipment can vary from a sheet of heavy glass to the neat Paterson frame, showing negative edge numbers and allowing space for annotation. I must admit to admiring those photographers who find the time to file negatives and contact prints properly in folders, with everything captioned and dated for the benefit of future historians! I recently acquired such a set, consisting of theatre, opera and ballet pictures taken in Austria

Facing page top: Family photographs deserve equal if not greater effort than your other pictures. Bottom: A suggestion of nudity is frequently more effective than open display in a girl picture. Delicately balanced exposure and lack of fill-in was responsible for the subdued nature of this shot. Left: Coloured filter, soft focus and backlighting add romance to this carefully posed photograph. Below: A keen eye can turn even the snatched shot into an attractive picture.

PRINTING

Right: The light that the artist *required for his work proved eminently suitable for this portrait study. Even illumination allowed maximum detail to be recorded in the paintings. The easels were arranged so as to avoid the appearance of any disturbing reflections on the canvas. Plain, light-coloured walls and ceiling acted as perfect reflectors. Palette and tubes of paint were purposely left in shot, as these are essential tools of the artist's profession. Below: The cramped confines of a houseboat were made to look more spacious by using a wide-angle lens. Skylights provided adequate, if somewhat uneven, lighting.*
Below right: Paintings are not difficult to photograph, even the simple compact camera can be relied on to produce satisfactory results. Reflections are the major problem and you may have to adopt awkward angles of view to avoid these. Polarising filters can be used, but for best results a technical camera with full movements is essential.

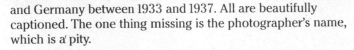

and Germany between 1933 and 1937. All are beautifully captioned. The one thing missing is the photographer's name, which is a pity.

BLACK AND WHITE

Black and white printing papers can be divided into four groups. Probably the most popular now is the resin coated type. With its dish or machine processing capability, short washing time and air drying ease, it would seem to be the answer to a photographer's prayer. Certainly, the speed at which a print can now be produced is appreciated by those who need a fast image. Glossy prints for reproduction are no longer a nightmare of glazing plates, eggshell crack marks, and solutions for the purpose with names like Bango. Even those of us who have not stayed up half the night, washing and drying the results of an evening's darkroom session, can understand the advantages that

resin coated papers offer. Indeed, with the advent of comparatively cheap processing machines, the wet bench and print dryer can almost be seen to be a thing of the past.

If this seems like a eulogy, then let me put RC paper into its proper perspective, for it does have some horrible disadvantages. Even in the pre-Bunker Hunt days, resin coated paper contained far less silver than its fibre-based contemporaries, with a consequent flattening of tones and indifferent blacks. Washing RC papers in a conventional sink requires great care, as the prints' sharp corners score the surface of each other. An RC print washer basket is to be recommended – particularly for a glossy surface. Another source of score marks is the use of a print squeegee or not perfectly clean chamois. Print dryer temperature must be kept low or blotches occur on a glossy surface.

Take care that the back of an RC print is also dry before stacking up a number of prints. Many conventional sepia toners

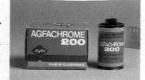

Top: A shop interior illuminated by fluorescent strip lights is a subject many photographers try to avoid. Accurate filtration is impossible, but the greenish cast can be reduced by using a Wratten CC30M or similar filter. Unless perfect colour fidelity is required, the use of filters is avoided in most interior situations.

PRINTING

do not work properly with RC's, though all the bleaches seem to. Knifing out black spots and tramlines is only possible on special Kodak RC paper. Mounting is a headache and requires special adhesives, and a special pen is needed to write captions on the back. I could go on about how it is not possible to pull or stew an RC print in a processing machine, in order partly to correct exposure error, but enough is enough.

Traditional fibre-based papers have also declined in silver content as well as popularity, to the extent that Kodak no longer market them. Those of us who still need single weight as well as double weight papers for artwork, re-touching, airbrush work, montages, captioning, etc, etc, are grateful that Ilford, Agfa and others still provide conventional bromide and warm tone Chlorobromide papers.

When it comes to a silver rich emulsion, they do make them like they used to – but at a price. Ilfords Galerie and Agfa Brovira are becoming increasingly popular with amateur and professional photographers alike. Compared with the price of resin coated papers, the premium for superb print quality is not very high. It is only in comparison to "ordinary" fibre-based bromide paper that the cost seems a bit high.

Multigrade resin coated paper is an old Ilford idea re-introduced in greatly improved form. A basic bromide emulsion is changed in contrast by the use of magenta and yellow filters, which allow a range of from grade 0 to grade 4, in half grade steps. Whilst the professional can purchase a dial-a-grade head for his enlarger, the amateur has to make do with a filter drawer and a set of grade filters. This may sound like a lot of effort, but any keen type will tell of running out of a certain grade of paper halfway through a printing session. With Multigrade this does not

happen. Furthermore it is possible, with practice, to use two grades of contrast on the same print, by craftily switching filters and making two exposures. Care must be taken not to move the enlarger head when swapping filters about. This is a scientific way of achieving the hotters, neaters, and huffing expertise of professional printers. (Hot water, undiluted developer and hot breath for increasing local development and contrast.) Multigrade shares the same advantages and disadvantages as other RC papers, except that at present it is priced roughly halfway between fibre and RC papers. A trial kit is well worth experimenting with. I know of several camera clubs, and other enthusiasts, who have switched completely to this ingenious system.

Full development has long been a technique of expert print makers. Manufacturers may well quote a time of 1½ to 2 mins at 68°F (20°C), but to extend this by a minute will ensure deeper blacks – even on resin coated paper. The shorter development time stated bears more relationship to the needs of processing machines rather than the highest possible print quality. To standardise on a 1½ minute development time assumes fresh developer, without taking into account oxidation or deposition of bromide from the development process. It is not that manufacturers are wrong, it is simply that their recommendations are based upon laboratory conditions and not upon practice. No manufacturers ever try to make two pints of developer last for an evening's printing session, and base their data sheets upon this.

A certain amount of simple chemical knowledge of the constituents of various paper developers will allow the enthusiast to ring the changes and/or match enlarger/negative characteristics to a combination of paper and developer. Most

3M 640-T, 640 ASA tungsten balanced colour
transparency film, available in 35mm size only.

paper developers are a combination of soft working metol or phenidone development agents, used in conjunction with hydroquinoné which performs the same function, but with much higher contrast. The term M.Q. is an abbreviation of Metol and Quinol – the latter being an ancient name for hydroquinone. Phenidone is a comparatively recent substitute for metol, as the latter can cause dermatitis. The first P.Q. developers proved to be unstable – a situation long since rectified. The proportions of metol and hydroquinone can be altered to produce a soft working, or a contrast, developer. The other constituents of a developer provide the final formula balance. Mild amounts of caustic soda are also used to increase contrast. Warm tone developers often contain amidol as the developing agent, in place of a metol/hydroquinone mix, though all three can be combined to produce a developer with a longer working life, as amidol goes off rapidly on its own. "Standard" MQ developers, like Kodak's D163 formula, can be used at slightly different dilutions in order to give a moderate degree of contrast control. D163 used at 1 part stock plus 2 parts of water, will give a brighter print. At this dilution strength, excessive development time can produce staining. Conversely, a solution working strength of 1 part stock plus 4 parts water, will produce a softer, slower working developer – but with a shorter dish life. These dilution tricks are useful when a print is either about half a grade too soft or hard, when developed in the recommended 1 plus 3 solution. As a guide, any "universal" MQ developer, which lists dilutions for both paper and films, may be used in a similar fashion to D163, after a little experimentation. Any print developer containing hydroquinone, should not be used at below 55°F (13°C), as hydroquinone becomes inert as a developing agent when too

Paradoxically, it is easier to produce night-time shots, albeit simulated, during the day than trying to capture the true effect at night. This is best done with the sun obscured or out of shot if a credible moonlight effect is required. Underexposure will generally need to be considerable; in the above example this was as much as four stops.

PRINTING

cold. Temperatures above 75°F (24°C) may cause a developer to stain prints, as well as being shorter lived.

COLOUR – POS/NEG AND POS/POS

Colour printing as a subject is a book in itself. I shall therefore limit myself to passing on a few hints which relate specifically to available light photography. The alternative is to let this little book reach tome proportions which as such would not be to the liking of the publisher – or, frankly, myself!

Until the "Video Still" – or Sony Mavica system comes of age, we are limited to printing from colour negatives, colour transparencies, or abrogating our photographic responsibilities and using 'instant' Kodak or Polaroid materials. Anyone who has tried colour neg/pos printing will, at first, be flummoxed by the "back to front" filter correction system. Simply, this is a matter of adding say, more blue filtration to correct a blue cast; whereas with printing from a transparency on to a reversal print material, one would logically (of course) contra-filtrate with yellow to remove blue. It is probably just a matter of where one's photographic education started, but nevertheless it is still easier to hold a correction filter over a print or tranny and say "That looks better," and filter accordingly. I should add, that a professional technique is to wave correction filters over the transparency or print until one strength is considered correct. When it comes to making the next Cibachrome, Ektachrome, Agfachrome or what have you, then half this filter value will be correct. The reason for this is that the eye will compensate more than a colour emulsion will. I have known colour negative printers, too, who use say a CP20 yellow filter visually over a too

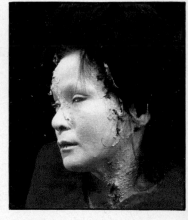

Photocalls or photography *during an actual performance are generally the province of the accredited professional. However, permission may sometimes be obtained for shots during a dress rehearsal. With absence of audience, camera angles may be less restricted, but silent operation is still the order of the day. Fast films are naturally useful in freezing the often frenetic movement, and they offer the added bonus of being tolerant of variable lighting.*

blue test print and then transpose to its complementary CP10 blue filter, to make the final corrected print. Those of you who are affluent, or manic enough to purchase a colour analyser, will of course not need this homespun tip, as electronic devices cannot be wrong.

One of the greatest snags to any colour printing process, is that there has been only one contrast grade available. However, as I pen these words, Agfa have announced a soft grade. This should help available light photographers tremendously. Until now, all colour print enthusiasts have been in the same primeval photographic situation as the old black and white printers, where subtle changes in technique and equipment were necessary in order to increase or decrease contrast. Perhaps the best analogy is in the tuning of a racing car engine. Each modification in itself is barely significant, but the sum total makes the difference between winning and losing a race.

I have already mentioned how to reduce contrast in an enlarger, by using a diffuser between light source and negative. Conversely the most contrasty enlarger is a traditional condenser enlarger. A good uncoated prewar enlarger lens is worth about the equivalent of a half grade loss in contrast. A modern three element coated quality lens will have higher contrast than a six element multicoated expensive lens. For modest degrees of enlargement, a mild plastic Cokin (or similar) lens diffuser, used over the lens for half the exposure will mix the highlights and the shadow areas with a consequent loss of contrast. Soft focus enthusiasts know all about this one.

Going from equipment to materials, most photographers know that a glossy print seems to give higher contrast and better colour saturation than a pearl or similar surface. It is also worth

experimenting with different maker's colour printing paper, utilising a 'standard' negative. Papers available from Kodak, U.S.A., Germany and Japan all have different characteristics. Much the same is true on the chemistry front. At a quick count, there are at least twenty colour paper developers available. Kodak and Agfa will no doubt be tops of the contrast league, but who is to say that the XYZ Manufacturing Co's product will not provide a valid contrast change alternative.

Obviously to try everything around will be expensive, it just depends on how keen you are. Certainly I know of professional colour printing labs who stock Kodak, Agfa and 3M paper, but only use one processing system. Working as they do for advertising agencies, print colours must match the actual product illustrated. Hence every trick in the book is sometimes necessary, particularly since packaging is now printed with new inks which contain fluorescins, that look one way and photograph another.

Such is the price of 'progress'.

The Cibachrome II and Kodak R14 processes for colour prints from colour transparencies, follow much the same fine tuning rules as pos/neg methods but with one exception. Cibachrome II can be used with alternative black and white first developers from the carefully researched Ilford formula. This is not to be recommended by either Ilford (or myself) except to those with a scientific bent. In no way will the cleverest 'boffin' improve on the work of Ciba's scientists, but he may well come up with a softer working and sometimes cheaper alternative. 'Ace' professional Cibachrome printers can achieve outstanding results with modified formulae and techniques. This degree of expertise is, however, beyond the range of normal mortals' pockets and ability, so should best be regarded solely as a source of inspiration and admiration.

DUPES AND COPYING

There are lots of reasons for any photographer to own some sort of slide duplicating equipment, whether it is a question of 'saving' an under-exposed transparency; cropping closer; correction of colour cast; providing extra transparencies for friends; making inter-negatives from transparencies for the same reason; black and white negatives from colour transparencies; or just for fun. The list can certainly be long enough to justify the outlay for extra equipment! I know several lecturers and business executives, who make up their own slide presentations. In both cases, this allows a greater number of slides to be made within the university or company budget, with a consequently more effective lecture or presentation.

The equipment necessary for duping can range from the crude to the sophisticated, with a corresponding price range. At the bottom end, a cheap bellows duplicating unit, using daylight, flash or flood, will cost about the same as a standard 50mm f1.8 lens. At the other end of the scale, you are talking about equipment with built-in electronic flash and contrast control, costing around the same price as a top of range Canon or Nikon with f1.2 lens – and you still need an expensive lens as well on top of this.

I cannot emphasise enough that, for consistently successful dupes, some sort of standardised equipment layout is essential. Also keep to one type of film – and the same processing laboratory – if you are not a do-it-yourselfer. Having purchased your equipment, run a test film on a wide variety of transparencies and make notes. The second test film should be an exercise to try and correct all the errors in the first. If in doubt, try several exposure and filter combinations. Again make notes. The third film should provide all the answers.

When my company went into the audio-visual business, we did just this. The results were put into black card mounts and fully annotated. These are always available for reference, thus providing a guide for any job that may come in. At a conservative estimate, well over 90% of originals are duped satisfactorily at the first attempt. If you do the same thing, don't forget to add bellows extension into the written data.

The cheapest form of duplicating equipment consists of a simple bellows unit, which utilises the camera's standard lens in reversed position, plus daylight or a photographic tungsten lamp as the light source. This method has the advantage of using the camera TTL metering system. It also has the disadvantage that the colour of daylight is not consistent: nor is a tungsten lamp, which is subject to variations in colour temperature due to voltage fluctuations. I know one man who makes very successful dupes using tungsten lighting. His secret is that he doesn't start work until most people have gone to bed. Late at night, there are no peaks in demand upon the electricity supply. This saves him purchasing an expensive voltage regulator in order to achieve consistent results.

At around the same level of expenditure are those transparency duplicators with a built-in lens. Most of these allow for a degree of cropping of the original – usually between a half and a quarter of the transparency area can be 'enlarged' to full frame. Optical quality of the built-in lenses can only be described as adequate, but these units are ideal for producing say, a colour inter-negative from a transparency, when only a postcard print is required as an end result. When working on a strict budget, there is a lot to be said for a simple bellows unit, with transparency holder, and, using a medium quality enlarger lens as a cost/ quality compromise.

Utilising a cheap electronic flash at a fixed distance from the transparency, in order to give some degree of exposure consistency, was another Spiratone introduction. At the top end of the scale there are units like the Bowens Illumitran, with a built-in electronic flash, metering from the focusing lamp, and in the more expensive model, a variable contrast control unit. My original Illumitran is now seven years old, has done a colossal amount of work and has only been serviced once for a very minor fault. Considering it has been in almost daily use during this time, I cannot recommend it highly enough. On the other hand it is an expensive toy if you cannot justify professional throughput.

When it comes to a choice of lens for your duping set-up, most of us will consider using our camera's standard lens. As mentioned in the close-up chapter, this is not a good idea unless the lens is used reversed. Again, even with this technique, an f2 or f1.8 lens is likelier to be a better performer than an f1.4 or f1.2. Any manufacturer's macro lens will be vastly superior, but does assume that the outlay can be justified. A modestly priced enlarger lens, like the Minolta Rokkor, will produce excellent dupes at considerably lower cost. Top quality enlarger lenses like the Nikon Nikkors, Leitz Focotar, Rodenstock Rodagon and many others, only really show their superiority when it comes to duping typographic slides, or those with very fine detail in the subject.

When it comes to a choice of camera for duping, there are unfortunately a couple of inherent SLR design disadvantages which must be considered. Most 35mm SLR's have a pessimistic focusing screen area. In practice, this can amount to equating what you see on the screen with what you get in a mounted Kodachrome. Some other slide mounts show rather more of the original transparency, which means that areas deliberately cropped out now appear in the final transparency. Either find a maker of slide mounts whose transparency area matches your camera, or alternatively buy an old Nikon F, F2 or Canon F1 which shows around 98% of actual transparency or negative area in the viewfinder. For this reason, my studio owns a large number of Nikon F's – to keep us going for many years to come. If you settle for an horizontal duping set-up, you will spend a considerable amount of time crawling around the table top on your knees. A vertical set-up can require a ladder – or waist-level viewfinder facility on your camera. Should you go beyond simple duping into the audio-visual field, a checked focusing screen is essential, in order to line up 'typo' slides.

Before moving on to emulsions, there are a couple of techniques for duping which may appeal to the impecunious, or those with only a spasmodic interest. Firstly, it is possible to produce just passable dupes by photographing a projected image from a screen. The camera should be as near to the projector axis as possible. It is preferable to use a beaded screen to avoid

illumination fall-off. You will probably need a CC 05 Red filter to negate the green cast caused by glass projector condensers – and, of course, use artificial light balanced film; or a correction filter on daylight stock. Most modern tungsten-halogen projector lamps give a 3200° K colour temperature balance. I have used this technique to produce ciné film titles. The second duping method involves the use of an enlarger, to produce an enlarged, or same-size, transparency or inter-negative, from a 35mm, 2¼" or 6 x 7cm transparency. This has the advantage of using sheet film, which means a single exposure can be made at any time. If your enlarger has a filter drawer, use a piece of matt acetate sheeting to soften the light source. Alternatively a circular piece of perspex can be placed above the condensers. Do not use opal glass – except for black and white work, as this has a pink tinge, which can be difficult to filter out in colour dupes. Metering for

Above: Used at dusk, daylight balanced films can produce pleasing and natural effects. *Facing page top left and bottom right: The green cast caused by fluorescent tubes, and some types of street lamps, cannot be filtered out effectively, but a complementary magenta* *filter will help reduce the effect.* *Top right: The colours of illuminated signs will appear more intense if slightly under-exposed.* *Bottom left: Fairgrounds are a popular subject with available light photographers.*

this method can be by a hand held exposure meter, providing it has a lockable reading. Alternatively, use an enlarger exposure meter or an SLR with a 90° lens attachment. In either case a

Kodak Ektachrome 200. 200 ASA daylight-balanced
colour transparency film. Available in 35mm.
120 rolls available in professional film.

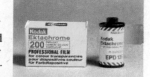

ertain amount of exposure testing needs to be done before a
meter or camera can be 'recalibrated'. As a guide, a Lunasix meter
ith incident light attachment, needs to be set at around 10,000
SA, yes, ten thousand – in order to provide a direct exposure
eadout, which relates to the enlarger lens aperture, when using
SA 25/32 Tungsten Ektachrome for duping. It is advisable to
se exposures of not less than 3 to 5 seconds with any enlarger,
s this allows for the lamp to warm up to a reasonable colour
emperature.

Which emulsion should one use for dupes? I would
commend the lower contrast Kodak colour films like EPD/EPT

Ektachrome or Kodachrome for transparencies, Vericolor for
colour negatives from transparencies, and Ilford HP5 or FP4 for
black and white negatives from transparencies. I am sure that
other makers' films could prove just as suitable: I simply haven't
tried them all in recent years.

There are special colour internegative materials made in
both sheet film and 35mm format. The latter can be purchased
only in bulk lengths generally, though I understand that some
retailers do market ready loaded cassettes. It is possible to load
your own cassettes (not Kodak) with any length you like, or use
reloadable cassettes which are still made by Nikon and others.

DUPES & COPYING

Felt lipped cassettes should only be re-used once – in the interests of safety. Most professional photographers and labs will throw once used cassettes in your direction – if you ask nicely. This special internegative film varies in colour balance and speed from batch to batch, so some initial tests are a must. Having said this, the lower contrast of this material has a tremendous advantage where real quality dupes are concerned. Bulk film should be kept in a refrigerator. This can extend its life up to about two years.

Rather than use a special duping film, there is a technique known as flashing, or pre-exposure, which, though more complex does achieve similar results. What this amounts to is to give a first exposure of the duping set-up light source with subject transparency removed, followed by the normal exposure with transparency replaced. The first exposure should be about one hundredth that of the second, which is usually achieved by the use of neutral density filters. One hundredth the exposure amounts to a six and a half stop reduction from the 'normal' exposure. Those of you who dupe by tungsten light, rather than electronic flash, can achieve this ratio by using higher shutter speeds as well as smaller stops. An accurate double exposure facility on your camera is essential.

Black and white negatives from colour transparencies are easy to produce. Contrast reduction can be achieved by over-exposing one stop and reducing development by 20%. However, should you not wish to do this or to try the pre-exposure technique, I have heard of photographers using a very light fog filter to reduce contrast. I suspect this is done with ciné fog filters, which are available in a greater range of strengths. Certainly the lightest fog filter I own is far too strong. Don't forget that other filters can be used to enhance a blue sky or to change tonal rendition. These can be placed over either lens or light source. Allow for the same filter factor as with a normal subject.

Sooner or later, you will find a transparency that will not duplicate satisfactorily, no matter what you do. The chances are that you are trying to dupe an Agfacolor transparency on to Ektachrome, or vice versa. For various obscure technical reasons, the makers' dyes are not compatible with each other in transmission wavelength, even though both can look the same to

Walls, ceilings and floors *colour the light they reflect. Even if you can't see the effect, your film can. Add to this the commonly encountered problem of mixed lighting and you will appreciate some of the difficulties of photographing interiors by available light. Unfortunately, unless you are prepared to compromise under such circumstances – give up.*

the eye. This effect doesn't happen with colour negative or print emulsions which can be swapped around quite happily.

CONCLUSION

I had scribbled out the last chapter, made a Xerox copy, and delivered it for typing. "That's that job jobbed", I thought, "now I can relax for a while before starting on the next book." An unread pile of photographic monthlies seemed a good way to unwind. Yet, by the end of an evening's browsing, I felt that so much had happened since I began, that a major re-write was necessary. The current acceleration of photographic technology is such that any book will be out of date as soon as it is printed – if not before.

Some of the new introductions will not necessarily help an available light photographer to take better pictures, but may well make his photographic life more convenient or interesting. Most of us are only too happy to try out a new product, and, if we like it, stay with it. There is an emerging pattern that all new colour materials are Kodak C41 or E6 compatible. Even though this means that Kodak's rivals have to pay a royalty, it does give them a world wide processing and printing facility through the labs set up for the Kodak processes. Agfa, Fuji, Konishiroku (Sakura) and 3M are all out for a bigger slice of Kodak's film and paper market share.

Whatever the machinations of the photographic industry, this can only help photographers by giving us a greater choice. The new "E6" Agfa sheet and rollfilm is a very worthy adjunct to Kodak materials. Its 100 ASA speed, fine grain, warmer colour rendering and lower contrast have already endeared it to some former Ektachrome users. This is not to say that it is better than the Kodak product, simply that as an alternative it can produce a more pleasing rendition of certain subjects.

Kodak, by introducing an ASA 200 Ektachrome sheet film, have given the large format user yet a further option in speed, colour rendition and contrast. Now if 3M were to produce their 640T emulsion in 10 x 8 sheet film form......!

Agfa have introduced VARIO-XL in rollfilm form, to give medium format users a combination of 1600 ASA capability with fine grain: surely something that would have seemed impossible before the advent of Chromogenic technology.

On the colour print front, there is Cibachrome II and Kodak Ektaflex, the latter being a sandwich together and peel apart process, which is available in both positive to positive and negative to positive forms. From the initial reviews, it would appear to provide a very much easier and quicker method of making occasional colour prints.

Few of the recent equipment introductions are really pertinent to this book, but is this certain? The Pentax autofocus camera could, for instance, make focusing in the dark easier – particularly if an optical or frame finder was added in order to facilitate composition. The solar powered Ricoh SLR could overcome battery deficiencies, provided it had had a good charge during the day! The revised Canon FI, Nikon updates and the spate of higher ratio zoom lenses, will certainly make picture-taking easier under any circumstances.

For the future, there is the Sony Mavica electronic technology, which, if combined with a miniaturised image intensifier could well make available light techniques a thing of the past. However, until electronic imagery can equal its silver based rival in terms of definition, colour fidelity and gradation, there is still much enjoyment to be had out of "squeezing an eighth at f2."

ACKNOWLEDGEMENTS

The publishers would like to express their
grateful thanks for the technical information
and for the loan of equipment to:

Canon (UK) Limited
Fotadvise (MEW) Limited
Hanimex (UK) Limited
Hasselblad (UK) Limited
Kodak Limited
Konishiroku UK

Leeds Camera Centre Limited
E. Leitz (Instruments) Limited
Minolta (UK) Limited
Nikon (UK) Limited
J. Osawa & Company Limited
Olympus Optical Company (UK) Limited

Pelling & Cross Limited
Photax (London) Limited
Polaroid (UK) Limited
Rank Photographic Limited
Vivitar (UK) Limited

169

Published by **CHARTWELL BOOKS, INC.** A division of **BOOK SALES, INC.**
110 Enterprise Avenue, Secaucus, New Jersey 07094
© 1982 Illustrations and text: Colour Library International Ltd., Guildford, Surrey, England.
Colour separations by FERCROM, Barcelona, Spain.
Display and text filmsetting by Acesetters Ltd., Richmond, Surrey, England.
Printed and bound in Barcelona, Spain by JISA-RIEUSSET & EUROBINDER.
ISBN 0 89009 557 4

D.L.B.: 31224